BLACK
CATS &
EVIL EYES

By the same author:

A Certain Je Ne Sais Quoi: Words We Pinched From Other Languages

One For Sorrow: A Book of Old-Fashioned Lore

Michael O'Mara Books Limited

First published in Great Britain in 2012 by
Michael O'Mara Books Limited
9 Lion Yard
Tremadoc Road
London SW4 7NQ

A CIP catalogue record for this book is available from the British Library.
Papers used by Michael O'Mara Books Limited are natural, recyclable products made from wood grown in sustainable forests. The manufacturing processes conform to the environmental regulations of the country of origin.

ISBN: 978-1-84317-887-3 in hardback print format
ISBN: 978-1-84317-916-0 in EPub format
ISBN: 978-1-84317-915-3 in Mobipocket format

1 3 5 7 9 10 8 6 4 2

Designed and typeset by www.glensaville.com,
from an original page design by Ana Bježančević

Printed and bound in Great Britain by Clays Ltd, St Ives plc

www.mombooks.com

CONTENTS

For Mum and Dad

INTRODUCTION

One of the most powerful things about superstitions is the way they have become engrained in the public consciousness. Passed on by word of mouth from one generation to the next and cemented in our minds by repetition and corroboration, irrational beliefs can hold startling authority. So much so that even if we don't actually believe in them in our rational minds, we follow them because gut instinct tells us we should, or, as was more often the case in the past, because we're too scared of the consequences if we don't.

Superstition is generally defined as an irrational belief that magic, luck or supernatural forces have the power to influence your life, or that actions that aren't logically linked to an outcome may have an effect on it. Such beliefs tend to be held most ardently when people find themselves at the mercy of chance. The human survival instinct tells us to seek a solution if our lives are threatened and our bodies naturally equip us with the ability to fight or flee. For our ancestors living in an age without proper sanitation, a guaranteed supply of basic food and clean water or modern medicine, so many of the menaces they faced were utterly beyond their control. They couldn't fend off the waves on a sinking ship, outrun the plague or fight the frost that would ruin the harvest, so they searched for other ways to save themselves: sailors cutting off their hair as an offering to the gods so that the sea would spare them; medieval Londoners applying dead pigeons to buboes in the desperate hope of curing bubonic plague; a farmer leaving fertile land uncultivated to protect a swallow's nest in case disturbing it caused his family to starve.

This book delves into the stories behind some of the superstitions that are still well known today, as well as exploring some of the most fascinating beliefs that have become less familiar in the modern age. Their origins are wide ranging, derived from either classical thought, religious ritual or rural wisdom. The focus is on those inspired by the hardships faced by everyday people in a time when life was 'nasty, brutish and short,' so they mostly fall into the categories of death omens (now signs of bad luck), charms against evil or witchcraft, and rituals surrounding births, deaths and other dangerous times.

Like much folklore, superstitious beliefs were usually passed on by word of mouth, so written records can be hard to come by. In many cases several centuries passed between their first appearance in print and subsequent references, which presents a challenge to folklorists attempting to trace their evolution. However, there is enough on record to help the interested amateur gain some understanding of where many of our most mysterious beliefs stem from.

To understand the superstitions collected in this book in context, we must imagine ourselves in a world vastly different from our own. Those beliefs that date back to antiquity evolved in an era steeped in the mythology of a pantheon of gods with human flaws vying with each other for power, and where Fate might triumph over even the most formidable deity. Humans saw themselves as pawns in the games of the gods and powerless in the face of their own predetermined destinies. Ritual governed their lives not so much because they were superstitious, but because that was the custom of their day.

The many beliefs that took hold during the Middle Ages, and in the sixteenth and seventeenth centuries, did so against a backdrop of extremism unrecognizable even in this post 9/11 age. The often hysterical fear of witchcraft that swept through Europe (and later America) plays a central role in the histories of many of the superstitions examined here. One particularly resonant medieval manuscript offers an illuminating insight into the beliefs of those times. *The Gospelles of Dystaues*, or *Distaff Gospels*, written in 1470 and translated into English in 1507, documented for the first time the wisdom of French peasant women. The book illuminates, for example, our distrust of giving a knife as a gift, our belief that a pregnant woman should be given what she craves and our fear that a howling dog is an omen of death. The women's testimonies were documented before the persecution of wise women as witches began in earnest, so they detailed the charms and remedies they used with a freedom that is heart-breaking in light of the torture and murder of the witch hunts that followed.

The problem these 'old wives' faced was that their beliefs fell outside the accepted religious framework of their time. For all its rituals and belief in the supernatural, the medieval Church would not tolerate this 'other' kind of wisdom, and this was in keeping with religious authorities throughout history. Even the Ancients made a distinction between religious ritual and superstitious practice. The first-century Roman poet Ovid describes many of the mores of his day and uses the word 'superstition' in much the same, faintly pejorative, way we do today to refer to those practices that were viewed as excessively credulous, whimsical or irrational.

This is one of the most fascinating things about looking back over the superstitions that have their origins in folklore. On the whole, they started out not as superstitions but as practices that were in keeping with the religious code or social norms of the time. They have come to be seen as superstitious only as our understanding of the world has deepened. If you carried a rabbit's foot to ward off digestive trouble in Roman times, for example, you did so because it was what your physician recommended. If you carried one in the 1600s, like the diarist Samuel Pepys, you might have done so because although you knew it was mere 'fancy,' it had worked for a respected friend and seemed also to have the desired effect on you. If you carry one today it's probably attached to some sort of 'good luck' key ring in the shape of a four-leaf clover with a horseshoe dangling from it, and you hold on to it either because your grandmother gave it to you on her deathbed or because you are extremely superstitious.

Following the same pattern of development, it's easy to see how the religious observances of the ancient Romans became the superstitions of the early Middle Ages, and how the Devil-defeating practices of the medieval peasant became the derided old wives' tales of the rationalist eighteenth century. What is really remarkable is that the seismic cultural shifts that have taken place over the centuries haven't eradicated superstition entirely. In fact, if you take superstition to include beliefs in the supernatural beyond the religious norm of the time, we are much more superstitious now than we were two hundred years ago, when the combination of scientific achievement and authorized religion kept the vast majority of people's beliefs within the mainstream. People have since begun to turn back to ancient healing methods like acupuncture, reiki and reflexology, and to the plant cures first used in Classical times. Twenty-first-century spiritualism and neo-paganism in all its forms are on the rise, and – in the West, at least – conventional religion plays the smallest role it ever has in human history.

Perhaps in this post-scientific-revolution era we are more accepting of the idea that not everything is within our understanding, which makes learning about the superstitions held by previous generations so appealing. We know about self-determination and that luck is just a string of probability equations, but we can't help but feel that there's something more to it. We know what happens to our bodies when they're buried and how age and diseases cause us to die, and yet many of us still have faith in some kind of afterlife or rebirth of the soul. No matter how certainly we know that the spirits of the damned aren't lurking under ladders hoping that we might sneeze at just the right moment for them to take possession of our bodies, something makes us change our path and look around for someone to say 'Bless you.'

CHLOE RHODES

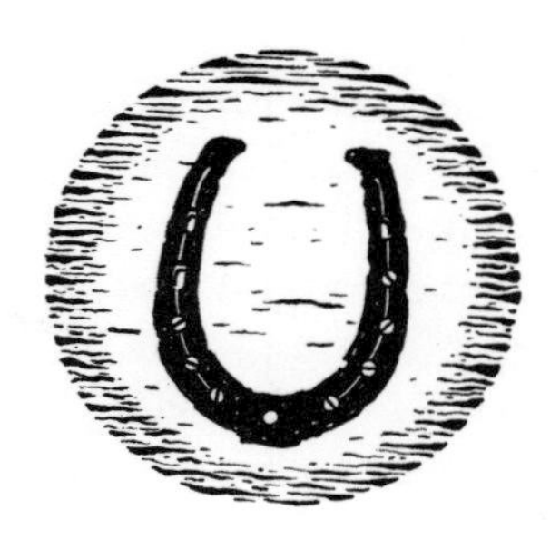

HORSESHOES

Horseshoes can be found hanging above the doors of homes across the world and are thought to ward off evil. One source of this belief in the Western world is described in *The True Legend of St Dunstan and the Devil,* written in 1871 by Edward G. Flight, which tells the story of a first-century blacksmith monk who later became the Archbishop of Canterbury and one of England's best-loved saints. Legend has it that during his days in the foundry, Dunstan was asked by a man to make some horseshoes for his own feet. As Dunstan prepared the man's feet for shoeing, he noticed that they were cloven hoofed and realized with horror that his customer was the Devil. Exhibiting a fearlessness befitting a future saint, he drove the nails into the soft centre of the hoof, causing the Devil so much agony that from that day on he didn't dare to go near a horseshoe.

The protective power of the horseshoe, however, pre-dates not only St Dunstan but Christianity itself. Hindu texts use the Sanskrit word 'Yoni' to describe the sacred temple or womb, representative of the Goddess Shakti, which was believed to be the origin of all life and is depicted in ancient stone carvings, paintings, and architecture as a downward-pointing horseshoe. It was also an important pagan symbol, representing the crescent moon and the ancient moon goddesses Artemis and Diana. In Arabic countries the horseshoe is incorporated into amulets that protect against the Evil Eye (*see* separate entry below), while in British, Celtic and Germanic folklore a horseshoe nailed above the door was used to defend homes from witchcraft.

In the West, as the more secular idea of bringing 'good luck' has taken precedence over the need to ward off evil, the positioning of the horseshoe has become significant. In the UK and the US they're most often hung with the open end up, to stop the good luck from falling out, though folklore traditionalists warn that this encourages trouble-making pixies to use them as seats, so open end up but tilted slightly is optimal. In the rest of the world the open end is usually down, mirroring the shape of the sacred womb. Whichever way a horseshoe is hung, more luck can be gleaned by keeping it in place with seven screws.

PICKING UP PENNIES

This tradition comes from a nursery rhyme that we commonly recite as 'See a penny, pick it up; all day long you'll have good luck.'

In fact the original rhyme featured pins, not pennies: 'See a pin and pick it up, all day long you'll have good luck. See a pin and let it lie, you'll feel want before you die.' This may in turn be derived from the old English proverb 'He that will not stoop for a pin will never be worth a pound,' which was first recorded in print in Samuel Pepys's *Diary* in 1668.

It is one of many ancient sayings to promote the notion that it's worth taking trouble over small things. People who used the rhyme in the 1600s would also have been fearful of leaving a pin on the ground because of their associations with witchcraft.

Pins were thought to have been used to bind a spell in place or to fix a desire – for good or ill, to an object that represented the person on whom the spell was being cast.

If you didn't pick up the pin, a witch might find it instead and use it in a spell against you.

Pins were also used in hexes, which could be performed to reverse the effects of damaging spells, often held responsible for the misunderstood medical ailments that afflicted citizens of the seventeenth century. Urinary infections, for example, were frequently 'treated' by placing pins representative of the patient's pain into a glass 'witch bottle' along with a sample of their urine. The mixture would be boiled to transfer the pain from the victim of the spell back to the witch. The bottle would then be buried or bricked up into the walls of the person's home to defend them against future curses.

The superstition had more mundane foundations too as pins were an essential tool for needlework, which was a necessity rather than a hobby in the seventeenth-century home.

The switch from pin to penny seems to have occurred in early nineteenth-century America and may have simply been a linguistic slip, although the appearance of the words 'In God We Trust' on American pennies is believed in some quarters to have transformed a castaway coin into a token of luck from the Good Lord for those who believe in him.

WALKING UNDER LADDERS

This superstition is one of the most widely adhered to of the modern age and one of many that have been appropriated over time by the Church. While many of the beliefs we might call superstitions today have their roots in the practice of religion, the Church itself holds that superstition is sinful, marking a deviation from worship of one God and giving credence to the occult.

The practice of walking around ladders, however, is deemed not to warrant the label of superstition since it is done in the interests of preserving something the Bible itself calls sacred. A ladder placed on level ground and leaning against a wall forms a triangular shape and the triangle was sacred because it represented the Holy Trinity of the Father, the Son and the Holy Spirit. Walking through the centre of a triangle was akin to breaking the Holy Trinity and violating God, which was blasphemous and therefore sinful. In fact, the triangle has been symbolic of life since ancient Egyptian times and disrupting a sacrosanct symbol was seen by the earliest civilizations as tempting fate. Even in our secular age it seems like an unnecessary risk to walk under a ladder from which a pot of paint or scaffolder who's lost his balance might easily fall.

There is an alternative source for this superstition however – the medieval gallows. Until the late 1800s the 'short drop' method was used for hangings, which meant that prisoners were hanged from a cart or simply made to step off a ladder with the hangman's noose around their neck, which usually resulted in death by strangulation. Later, when new drop gallows were introduced, which caused a quicker death by breaking the prisoner's neck, ladders were propped against them so that prisoners could climb the scaffold ready for the drop. These were used again by the executioner when the bodies were collected. It was widely believed that the souls of those who'd been executed loitered under the ladder (since their crimes made them unfit for heaven) so it was inviting misfortune of the most grisly kind to walk underneath one and mingle with them.

SPILLING SALT

Until relatively recently, salt was one of the most precious commodities known to man. The location of salt mines determined where cities would flourish, salt routes paved the way for later trade routes and, before refrigeration, curing with salt was the primary method by which food could be preserved, so lives depended on it. Without mechanized techniques for mining rock salt or the means by which to evaporate enough salt water to extract sufficient quantities of sea salt, it was expensive and hard to come by. All of this meant that it was unlucky in the most straightforward of ways to spill salt. As with so many superstitions that still influence our behaviour today, fear of the forces of evil shaped our responses to what might otherwise have been regarded as simple misfortune.

Salt was used in Greek and Roman religious ceremonies and is still used to make holy water in the Catholic Church so spilling it was seen as an act of the Devil. This notion is thought by some to have been cemented by the overturning of the salt cellar by Judas Iscariot during the Last Supper, as depicted in Leonardo da Vinci's masterpiece. In medieval times it was believed that the Devil waited behind your left shoulder for any opportunity to pounce, which gave rise to the tradition of throwing a pinch of salt over your left shoulder immediately after you spilled it to strike him in the face and prevent him from making further trouble.

In Norway it was believed that the more salt spilled the greater the misfortune would be as more tears would have to be shed in order to dissolve all the grains. In the Turkic states, ancient folklore held that a white angel lived at the right shoulder of every person and a black angel lived at the left shoulder; a pinch of the spilled salt in the eye of the black angel could prevent him from ruining future plans.

THE EVIL EYE

Belief in the power of the evil eye dates back to the earliest civilizations and references to it can be found aplenty in the writings of ancient Greek and Roman poets and philosophers including Aristophanes, Plutarch and Pliny the Elder. Put simply, it refers to the belief that those who possess the evil eye (sometimes described as a jealous spirit) can put a curse on others, usually unintentionally, by gazing at them enviously. The evil eye is usually developed in a person by their coveting of the good fortune of another. Biblical references also exist; Proverbs 23:6 reads 'Eat thou not the bread of him that hath an evil eye, neither desire thou his dainty meat.'

The effects of the curse vary slightly between cultures but the late American Professor of Folklore and Evil Eye expert Alan Dundes wrote that while belief in its powers spread through the Middle East, Africa and Europe – especially the Mediterranean region (with many variations in the methods used to avert it) – the feared effects of being given the evil eye tended to be similar: diseases related to dehydration, such as vomiting, wasting or shrivelling, sometimes resulting in death.

Young children are believed to be at greatest risk of the evil eye, perhaps since their beauty and innocence is most likely to attract envious glances. Praising the appearance of a child is also believed to attract the evil eye, so in many countries where belief in the curse is strong, it is customary touch a child immediately after praising it in order to remove the curse. In Bangladesh, mothers of young women who are particularly likely to attract the envy of others through their beauty put a black kohl mark behind their daughter's ear to counter ill effects. In the Middle East and in some Mediterranean countries, glass amulets showing a blue eye are worn on jewellery or hung over doorways to repel the eye's power. Blue eyes are regarded as evil in these countries because they aren't usually found within the local population, and the belief is likely to have been underlined by the propensity of blue-eyed tourists to these areas for failing to recognize that photographing or cooing over children is frowned upon.

Jewish tradition protects children from the eye by tying a piece of red string around their wrists. In Italy, where the curse is also believed to affect men and cause impotence, a hand gesture that uses the fingers as horns is used to counter it. These days, such preventive measures are usually judged to be effective, though in past times the prevalence of diseases causing dehydration in young children meant that many deaths were put down to the influence of the evil eye.

MOONLIGHT

As the closest and brightest aspect of the night sky, the moon has held humankind in its thrall since the earliest civilizations.

Although the ancients had no notion of the gravitational influences the moon exerted on our planet, they did believe that the moon controlled all the water on the earth, and that not only the oceans but also the fluids within their bodies were acted on by the moon. The word 'lunatic,' from the Latin *lunaticus,* meaning moonstruck, was used to describe those who seemed to be sent temporarily mad by a full moon and was in use in English from the early fourteenth century. In 1393, William Langland's allegorical poem *Piers Plowman* refers to 'Lunatic lollers and lepers about,' more or less mad according to the moon's phases.

In the days before neuroscience had shed light on the intricate workings of the brain, people suffering from brain disorders such as epilepsy were thought to be afflicted by a madness brought on by the waxing and waning of the moon. This belief gave rise to strong superstitions surrounding the power of the moon: to sleep in moonlight was thought to cause insanity or 'moon-blindness' and special care was taken to draw the curtains against a full moon. It was also considered dangerous to look at the moon in a mirror, or to stare at it for too long when it was full. These beliefs became further entrenched in the Middle Ages, when stories about werewolves and vampires combined with an unshakeable belief in the influence of the Devil to feed popular fear about the power of the moon. All kinds of inexplicable behaviour was attributed to its influence: 'It is the very error of the Moone,' wrote Shakespeare in *Othello*. 'She comes more nearer Earth than she was wont, And makes men mad.'

Some of us still blame a full moon for unusual antics; it has been linked to a rise in the number of suicides, hospital admittances and crime, and although there are no scientific studies to prove it, the police have reported an increase in aggressive behaviour on nights when the moon is full – some British police forces even employ extra officers to cope with the surge.

BREAKING A MIRROR

The widely held superstition that breaking a mirror means seven years' bad luck dates back to the late eighteenth century, but the idea that death or some other misfortune will befall anyone who breaks a looking glass goes back much further. The Romans, alongside ancient Greeks, Chinese, Africans and Indians believed that the soul of a person was transferred into their reflected image when they looked into a mirror. If the glass was damaged, the soul held within it would be too. In his 1777 publication *Observations on the popular antiquities of Great Britain*, the English antiquarian John Brand wrote 'the breaking a Looking Glass is accounted a very unlucky accident. Mirrors were formerly used by Magicians in their superstitious and diabolical operations; and there was an antient [*sic*] Kind of Divination by the Looking Glass.'

As with many superstitious portents of doom, the exact nature of the misfortune that lies ahead has evolved over time. When Alfred, Lord Tennyson referred to it in his poem 'The Lady of Shalott' in 1842, the result was a generalized misery: 'The mirror cracked from side to side; "The curse has come upon me," cried the Lady of Shalott.'

By later in the 1800s a broken mirror foretold a death in the family or the loss of a friend, and the first reference to seven years of bad luck appeared in print in 1851. The exact origins of this very specific period of strife are uncertain, but may be linked to the Roman belief that the human body renewed itself every seven years and perhaps this process of renewal provided a clean slate for the soul.

These days, while we still fear the curse of a broken mirror, few of us do more than sweep up the pieces and hope no one's noticed, but our forefathers practised a range of rituals to mitigate the disaster. Some ground the broken pieces to dust to release the soul trapped inside, others buried the shards beneath a tree by the light of the next full moon, and Africans working as slaves in America are reported to have believed the bad luck could be washed away by placing the shattered pieces in a southerly flowing river.

LOOSE OR BROKEN SHOELACES

It is generally held to be bad luck if your shoelace breaks or comes loose while you're walking along, but this seems not to be simply for the obvious practical reason that it might cause you to trip and fall, since a fuller version of the belief states that you must continue to walk another nine paces before retying a loose shoelace, otherwise you will tie bad luck to yourself for that day.

Tripping over or stumbling as you walk has been regarded as a sign of trouble ahead since Roman times. In 45 BC, the Roman philosopher and statesman Cicero in his philosophical treatise *De Divinatione* lists those things noted with superstition as 'stumbling, breaking a shoe-latchet, and sneezing.' Some attribute the superstition to the cautionary tale of the Roman Emperor Augustus who, according to legend, stumbled over the laces of his *caligae* sandals as he fled from an attempt on his life, only narrowly escaping assassination. The distrust of an untied lace deepened in seventeenth- and eighteenth-century

Europe, when men sporting even a well-tied, dandyish 'Oxford' shoe were felt to represent a decline in morality and masculinity in contrast to the sturdy buckle popular with more macho types.

As life became less precarious, omens that had once foretold death or disaster took on a lighter tone and a loose lace was said by young women to be a sign that your sweetheart was thinking about you. In less giddy circles it was thought that if the left lace was loose someone was speaking ill of you, while if the right came undone someone was singing your praises. It remained bad luck to dream of a shoelace becoming untied, though if a knot forms in a lace it's good luck.

To turn the bad luck into good you could take the shoe off completely and throw it in the direction of someone to whom you wish well. The traditional wedding good-luck superstition of tying shoes to the back of newly-weds' cars comes from a sixteenth-century tradition described by Proverb collector John Heywood in his *Dialogue of the Effectual Proverbs in the English Tongue Concerning Marriage* published in 1598: 'And home again hitherwards quicke as a bee, now for good luck, cast an old shoe after me.'

NEVER LEAVE A HOUSE THROUGH A DIFFERENT DOOR FROM THE ONE USED FOR ENTRANCE

As the entry point of the home and the threshold to the private world, the door has a special status in folklore. Talismans against evil have been mounted on doorframes since the earliest dwelling places were constructed, and to this day good-luck tokens like horseshoes, sacred statues or Chinese feng shui symbols can be found on front doors from East to West. In China, doors are often still painted with a fresh coat of auspicious red paint before New Year to bring good luck and happiness to the home.

These charms have their origins in the belief that

humanity lived under constant threat from the forces of evil. In the ancient world these forces were represented by fearful gods; Set or Seth, the demon of death in Egyptian mythology, or the fearsome winged monster Typhon in ancient Rome. In the Western world during the Middle Ages, the Devil was as much of a presence in everyday life as God, and was held responsible for the myriad of misfortunes that might befall a person living in times when the average life expectancy at birth was thirty-five years. Evil spirits in the form of sprites and fairies or demonically possessed animals might be lurking in every shadow; the home had to be defended from these destructive forces and the front door was the first line of defence. It was therefore considered unlucky when entering a house for the first time to use its back door, since it wasn't protected against evil spirits. Visitors were always asked to leave by the same door by which they'd entered in order to prevent them from taking the home owner's luck and protection out with them.

Doors were also seen as representative of less tangible barriers, so they were always opened after a death in the house to let the departing spirit out, and during a birth to let the soul of the new arrival in.

BLACK CATS

Black cats feature in the mythology of many cultures, and superstitions about them are still familiar to most of us in modern times. They are a prime example of the contrariness of many of our superstitious beliefs; some swear they're lucky, others see them as a sign of certain doom. According to Norse legend, Freya, queen of the Valkyries and goddess of fertility, drove a chariot pulled by black cats that some sources suggest turned into horses possessed by the Devil. In the Middle Ages, black cats were often portrayed as the familiars of witches, which is likely to be the origin of the distrust with which they are regarded in America, where early Puritan settlers rejected anything associated with the Devil and witchcraft. In the US it is still considered a bad sign if a black cat crosses your path, since it means you have been noticed by the Devil. In Germany the same rule applies if the cat is walking from right to left, but if it crosses from left to right then good fortune is coming your way. In Scotland the arrival of a black cat outside your home is a sign of coming prosperity, while in China black cats are regarded as harbingers of hunger and poverty. In Italy, if a black cat should rest on the bed of a sick person it is thought to signify the patient's imminent death.

In England a black cat is still considered lucky if it walks towards you, though there are countless variations and reversals of the rule across the world, the origins of which have become blurred and blended by the passage of time. The sixteenth-century English author William Baldwin's satirical work *Beware the Cat* put into print the belief, commonly held at the time of its publication in 1561, that cats were in fact witches disguised in animal form: 'A Cat hath nine lives, that is to say, a witch may take on her a Cat's body nine times.'

In Great Britain and Ireland though, it is considered lucky to own or see a black cat, particularly on important occasions such as weddings or at the start of a long journey. King Charles I was so convinced of his own black cat's luck-bringing qualities that he had it guarded round the clock. When it eventually died he was reportedly devastated that his luck had run out. Coincidentally (or not!) the king was arrested by Cromwell's troops the very next day and was beheaded two years later.

THE NUMBER THIRTEEN

There are few superstitions still so widely and publicly observed as the belief that the number thirteen is unlucky; high-rise buildings are constructed without a thirteenth floor, aeroplanes rarely have a thirteenth aisle and you'd be hard pressed to find a hotel room with the number thirteen on the door. The source of our distrust is held by most to be biblical: at the Last Supper, when Jesus told his twelve apostles that one of them would betray him, there were thirteen at the table and Judas was said to have been the thirteenth guest. (*See also* Friday 13th.)

There are numerous alternative explanations for our fear of the number, however, many of them equally well-rooted in our cultural history. Norse legend describes a banquet at which twelve gods were dining when a thirteenth guest Loki, a cunning, shape-changing god, arrived. The deities were entertaining themselves by throwing things at favoured god Balder, who they knew to be immune from injury, but Loki tricked the blind god Hod into killing Balder by throwing an arrow made from mistletoe, knowing it to be the one thing that could harm him. Balder's death was the start of Ragnarok, the end of the old world during which there were three years of winter and the Norse gods were all killed.

The roots of the 2012 'End of days' theories can also be linked to the number thirteen. In ancient Persia, where the twelve constellations of the zodiac were assigned to the calendar year, people believed that each sign reigned over the world for a millennium. Once each constellation had completed its rule and the thirteenth millennium began, there would be no dominant constellation, resulting in chaos.

For both ancient and modern scholars of sacred geometry exploring mathematical patterns and geometric forms in the natural world, the number thirteen is revered as a basic structural unit within nature and the heavens. There are thirteen major joints in the skeleton, the moon completes thirteen degrees of its orbit each day and there are thirteen lunar cycles in a solar year. The number is also auspicious in Judaism where it is the age of responsibility when a boy becomes bar mitzvah. Usually written as *yod-gimel,* thirteen is also the numerical value of the word *ahava,* meaning love. All of which has led some to suggest that our suspicion of the number might have its roots in anti-Semitism.

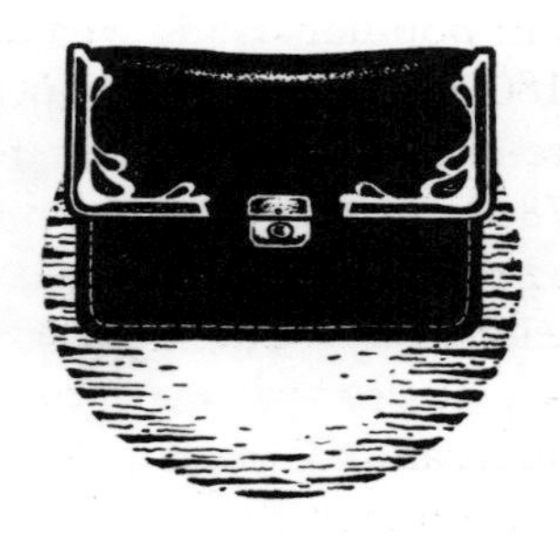

THE GIFT OF A PURSE OR WALLET SHOULD ALWAYS INCLUDE MONEY

The giving of presents is riddled with risk for the superstitious, since it's one of the few occasions when our own actions have a direct impact on others for good or ill.

According to folklore, an empty wallet or purse received as a gift will stay empty forever, so to give one is akin to cursing the recipient with a lifetime of poverty. The belief is thought to stem from the notion that the Devil would inhabit an empty purse and use poverty to drive people to acts of desperation such as theft, deceit and prostitution that were regarded as ungodly and sinful.

The superstition was strengthened by its association with a saying that dates back to at least the early eighteenth century, which states 'An empty purse is the Devil.' The phrase was in popular use in Britain and America throughout the 1800s and can be found in print in an essay written by the pre-eminent American lexicographer Noah Webster, Jr in 1786 lamenting the weakness of the federal government: 'It prevents the adoption of any measures that are requisite for us as a nation; it keeps us from paying our honest debts . . . It also throws out of our power all the profits of commerce, and this drains us of cash. Is not this the devil? Yes, my countryman, an empty purse is the devil.'

The same phrase appeared in an 1882 edition of *Notes and Queries*, a scholarly magazine devoted to the exploration of the English language, history and antiquarianism, and we still use a version of it today. 'The Devil Danced in Empty Pockets' is the title of a song by contemporary American country singer Joe Diffie, and the same line appears in Tom Waits's murder ballad 'Lucinda.'

To guard against the curse of the empty purse, it was customary from the 1800s onwards to keep at least one coin in a wallet, or, if that had to be spent, a piece of string or twine could be used to trick the Devil into keeping out. Many people still slip a coin, or, if they're in a generous mood, a note, inside a purse or wallet if it's to be a gift.

PARTING ON A BRIDGE

If you want to see a friend again, the full version goes, then don't ever say goodbye to them on a bridge. As with many old-fashioned superstitions, this one confers symbolic meaning on the physical world. Rivers divide bodies of land and the bridges that spanned them were seen as a kind of no-man's-land, belonging to neither bank and representative of separation. To part company from a friend on a bridge and each to set off for opposite banks of a river was therefore to risk being parted for ever, just as the land had been. The motives for adhering to this custom weren't simply the mirroring of nature; what really drove their reluctance to part ways over water was their fear of the Devil fuelled by folk tales.

In the legend of the Devil's Bridge in Cardiganshire, an old woman had become separated from her cow by a deep ravine and the Devil took advantage of her distress by offering to throw a bridge across in return for the soul of the first living creature to cross it. The old woman agreed and the Devil rubbed his hands with glee, delighted that in her panicked state of mind she'd been willing to sacrifice herself, but instead she took a crust of bread from her pocket and threw it across and her dog ran after it, angering the Devil. Similar stories are told in different parts of Europe; on the river Main in Frankfurt it's a bridge builder who drives a rooster across ahead of him; in Switzerland, the St Gotthard Pass is spanned by 'The Devil's Bridge,' named after a legend about the Devil waiting to catch anyone crossing after dark.

These tales have travelled down to us in more and more diluted forms until the accepted wisdom became that crossing any bridge after dark, or being the first to cross a bridge at any time of day, meant running a gauntlet of evil sprites, trolls (incorporating the Norwegian fairytale of the Three Billy Goats Gruff) or the Devil himself. In Marie Trevelyan's *Folk Lore of Wales* published in 1909 she writes: 'Very old people always spat thrice on the ground before crossing water after dark, to avert the evil influences of spirits and witches.' It became tradition to send an animal over a new bridge before the first human crossed and bridge builders would often leave placatory gifts of money bricked into the stonework. Even today it is still common for a new bridge to be officially 'opened' by an important figure in the community and for a bottle of wine to be smashed against its side to 'bless' all those who cross it.

OWLS

To the ancient Greeks, the owl was revered for its link to Athena, goddess of wisdom, justice and philosophy. Archaic art often shows the goddess with an owl called the Owl of Athena, or, under Roman rule, the Owl of Minerva perched on her head and according to Theophrastus, writing circa 319 BC, 'If an owl is startled by him in his walk, he will exclaim "Glory be to Athene!" before he proceeds.' We still associate owls with wisdom for this reason, although their wisdom also made them a creature to be feared for their prophetic powers.

Roman historian Pliny the Elder, writing in AD 77, believed they always brought bad news and described the bird as 'most execrable and accursed.' To hear one screeching is described as a portent of doom in works by Chaucer and Shakespeare, as well as in songs and poems passed on by word of mouth. One old rhyme from the southern United States is specific about the nature of the threat ahead:

When you hear the screech owl, honey,
in the sweet gum tree,

It's a sign as sure as you're born a death is bound to be;
Unless you put the shovel in the fire mighty quick,
For to conjure that old screech owl, take care the one that's sick.

The owl's perceived ability to foretell a death stems from the fact that as nocturnal birds, they were associated with night and the sinister spirits that were thought to roam the earth in the hours of darkness. Seeing an owl in daylight is thought to be especially bad luck and if one flies around and around the house it is a sure sign of the imminent demise of someone living within.

There are regional variations in our interpretation of the owl's call however; according to Welsh legend an owl hooting is a sign that a local woman has just lost her virginity. In Germany, if an owl's call is heard during childbirth then the child will be cursed with an unhappy life, while in France, a pregnant woman hearing an owl will know that her baby is a girl.

Whatever intelligence they bring, any bad luck associated with hearing or seeing an owl could be counteracted in the Middle Ages by thrusting irons (such as the shovel mentioned in the rhyme quoted above)into a fire or taking your clothes off and turning them inside out before swiftly dressing again. To ensure longer-term protection against the curse of hearing their hoot you could throw salt or vinegar into the fire to give the owl a sore tongue and silence it forever.

NEVER KILL A ROBIN

The robin redbreast, or European robin to give it its official title, is among the most beloved of gardener's companions. Sociable and bold, they seem unafraid of human contact and are easily tamed, which makes it easy to see why killing one is regarded as wrong. However, our concern for their welfare has roots in Christian folklore. Legend has it that as well as singing with all the other birds to soothe Jesus as he suffered on the cross, the robin also tried to remove the thorns from his head and its feathers became stained with Christ's blood as it did so. An alternative version of the origins of the red breast tells how a robin present in the stable where Jesus was born noticed that as Mary and her baby lay sleeping, the fire that was keeping them warm almost died out. The robin rekindled the flames by fanning them with its wings and was rewarded with its red breast by Mary when she woke, in recognition of its devotion.

Both versions cast the robin as good-hearted and

selfless and secured the bird its place as a folklore favourite. A rhyme featuring the robin from a collection of poems, songs and fables for children, *A Poetical Description of Songbirds* published in the US in 1773, sums up the esteem in which they were held: 'The robin and the jenny wren, are God Almighty's little cock and hen.' A similar sentiment is conveyed in William Blake's *Auguries of Innocence* by the familiar lines 'A robin redbreast in a cage,/Puts all heaven in a rage.'

Fear of 'heaven's rage' meant that most country people regarded it as extremely unlucky to kill a robin, even by accident. The repercussions for doing so vary from place to place but all are severe; some say the hand that snuffs out a robin's life will shake forever after, in Irish folklore a large, painful lump is said to appear on the right hand of anyone guilty of the sin, while in Yorkshire, it is thought that if a farmer is responsible for a robin's death, the milk his cows produce will turn the colour of blood.

NEVER KILL A SWALLOW

In the suburban areas of modern towns, swallows are often regarded as a nuisance. In Britain, swallows and their nests are fully protected under the Wildlife and Countryside Act of 1981, which makes it an offence to intentionally kill, injure or take any wild bird. Nonetheless, their clusters of mud nests can damage walls and eaves and numerous 'pest control' services make it their business to get rid of them once the birds have migrated. However, according to folklore, it is incredibly bad luck to kill a swallow. The English author Thomas Browne put his finger on the problem in 1650 in the fifth edition of his popular book *Vulgar Errors,* which addressed the superstitions of his day: 'Though useless unto us and rather of molestation, we commonly refrain from killing swallows, and esteem it unlucky to destroy them.'

Belief in the sanctity of the swallow stems from the fact that they were sacred to the Penates, or house gods of the ancient Romans, who watched over the home and store cupboard with some sources stating that they were thought to be the embodiment of these gods. The bird's perpetual flight fuelled the perception of them as spiritual creatures, especially during the Middle Ages, when the fact that they were never seen to land led many people to believe that they had no feet.

The birds are also important in Danish folklore, where they are known as the *svale,* the bird of consolation, a name given to them because they were said to have tried to comfort Jesus on the Cross by hovering above him and singing '*svale, svale!*,' which translates as 'cheer up, cheer up!'

In rural areas it's seen as lucky if a swallow makes its home in your roof as it is thought to confer protection from fire and storm damage. This particular belief probably originates from the observation that homes in which swallows nested were rarely harmed by the weather, as swallows seek out nesting spots that are naturally well protected from the elements. It is thought to be even luckier if one flies in through your door, though you should be wary if it abandons its home in a hurry, since misfortune is likely to be on the way. Farmers across Europe take particular care not to disturb swallows, believing that if they kill one the milk yield from their cows will suffer, or, if they disturb a nest, their harvest will be poor.

IT IS BAD LUCK TO LET MILK BOIL OVER

Milk was an important ingredient in the food of the Middle Ages, but because there was no refrigeration it didn't stay fresh for long. People kept only as much as they knew they would need, which naturally meant that it was seen as bad luck to let milk boil over and go to waste. The superstition has deeper roots than the need for frugality. There is evidence that since prehistoric times, tribal communities have believed in sympathetic magic – the idea that like produces like, so a yellow fruit might cure jaundice, and that two things which were once connected retain their connection, even after they have been physically separated.

These notions were first described by influential Scottish social anthropologist James Frazer in his book *The Golden Bough*, published in 1890, which compared mythology and religion across the world. The idea of the interconnectedness of two things can be most easily explained with an example: anything done to the milk of a cow, for instance, might be felt by the animal itself. In societies where the health and productivity of livestock determined the health and indeed the survival of the people who kept them, every precaution against an animal being harmed or falling ill was taken. Where the causes of death and disease weren't understood, they were often blamed on people's failure to adhere to the customs dictated by such superstitions. In the Europe of the Middle Ages this might have influenced people's anxiety about letting the milk boil over, while in many African tribes, including the Masai and Baganda of East Africa and the majority of tribes in Sierra Leone, it meant not boiling milk at all in case it hurt the cow and stopped it from producing.

NEVER KILL A SPIDER

Like many superstitions that have their roots in country customs, this one makes sense for practical reasons. Spiders are useful to farmers because they eat the aphids and other insects that can destroy a farmer's crops, so it was in the interests of rural people, especially those living in the days before pesticides, to preserve the life of this helpful creature. Spiders were welcomed in the home for similar reasons in that it was better to have a few cobwebs in the corners than for your food (which couldn't in those days be refrigerated) to become infested with flies. There are mythical sources for the superstition also, with one legend in varying forms, making the harming of spiders a taboo across cultures.

A Christian fable tells how a spider hid the baby Jesus as Mary and Joseph fled with him from King Herod's men. Joseph had found a cave high in the mountains where Mary could rest as they ran from Herod, who had ordered the killing of all male children under the age of two. The Roman army were close behind and began to search the caves, but when they saw an intricate spider's web across the entrance to the one in which Jesus lay sleeping they passed by, assuming that it must have been there, undisturbed, for many days.

The Torah tells the parallel story of how David, later the King of Israel, was saved by a spider's web covering the cave in which he was hiding from an army sent by the King Saul to kill him. In the story of the life of the prophet Mohammed is the tale of how he took shelter in a cave when fleeing his enemies and was saved when a tree sprouted in front of it and a spider built a web between the tree and the cave.

The spider's usefulness in protecting human life can be traced back even earlier; in AD 77 the Roman scholar Pliny wrote about the medicinal uses of spider's webs, which were mixed with vinegar and oil and used for healing fractures and cuts. These days we have fewer uses for our eight-legged friends but many of us still put them out the back door with trembling hands rather than risk bad luck by squashing them.

IT IS BAD LUCK TO PASS ANYONE ON THE STAIRCASE

It would lead to some fairly serious pedestrian traffic jams if we tried to adhere to this superstition on the stairways of office blocks, train stations and the shopping malls of the modern world. The best we can do to dispel any bad luck we incur is to keep our fingers crossed or hold our breath as we pass. In the mid-nineteenth century, however, our forefathers were doing their best to avoid it, probably because of the association between stairways and the pathway to heaven. One old English rhyme, passed down by word of mouth, states 'Never pass upon the stairs, you'll meet an angel unawares.'

In the mid-nineteenth century the living world was seen as much more closely linked to the spirit world than it is today. Despite the emergence of atheism in the previous century, most people still believed in the afterlife and in the ability of spirits who hadn't found rest to appear to the living. Accounts of hauntings from this era often describe ghostly figures on staircases: spectral women in white descending the stairs or the ghosts of dead children sitting on the steps.

There may also have been practical reasons for the superstition that stemmed from the narrowness of early staircases. Two people passing on the narrow staircases of fortified medieval castles would leave themselves open to attack from behind. These stairways were also booby-trapped with 'stumble steps' which were made different heights from the others in order to trip any attacker advancing up them.

An earlier piece of stairway folklore meant that by the sixteenth century anyone hoping to be married might have appreciated a stumble step, as it was considered lucky to stumble on your way up a staircase and was a good omen of a future wedding in the household. Stumbling on your way down was still thought of as a misfortune though and seen as a sign of bad luck to come. Restoration dramatist William Congreve recorded the belief in his 1695 play *Love for Love*: 'But then I stumbled coming down stairs, and met a weasel; bad omens those.'

NEVER TREAD ON A GRAVE

The Greek scholar Theophrastus (*c.*372–*c.*278 BC), who succeeded Aristotle at the Peripatetic School, wrote a study of human nature entitled *The Characters* that was made up of sketches of different moral character types. The English translation incudes among the traits of 'The Superstitious Man': 'He will not tread upon a tombstone.' Theophrastus's work was published in around 319 BC, but after the fall of the Roman Empire his teachings were lost to the Western world until the twelfth century, when translations of Latin texts began to be made. This superstition was incorporated smoothly into a medieval world in which the risk of dying young was enough to make anyone who valued life avoid anything that might increase their chances of going to an early grave.

Many of the superstitions surrounding the dead in this

period stemmed from the idea that the departing soul would loiter on earth for as long as possible before making its journey either upwards to heaven or downwards to hell. During this time of restlessness it would look for other souls to keep it company on its journey, so doing anything to antagonize the newly buried was seen as foolhardy in the extreme.(*See also* The Covering of Mirrors after a Death.)

By the eighteenth century the superstition had evolved so that a more generalized misfortune would befall anyone who walked on a grave. The English Romantic poet Samuel Taylor Coleridge puts it succinctly in his 1798 poem 'The Three Graves': 'To see a man tread over graves / I hold it no good mark; / 'Tis wicked in the sun and moon, / And bad luck in the dark!'

The belief remains prevalent in America and across much of Europe. In predominantly Catholic Brittany there is a walled cemetery at the Church of Lanrivoare where 7,727 'unnamed saints' are buried, which is so strict about the superstition that you can enter only after you have removed your shoes. Failure to abide by this rule is said to have once resulted in a visiting stranger falling backwards so that his entrails came out.

NEVER REMOVE FLOWERS FROM A GRAVE

Archaeologists believe that burial rituals can be traced back to the Middle Palaeolithic, when, in Europe, Neanderthals buried weapons alongside their dead. There is some evidence to suggest that plants and flower heads were buried with bodies in this era, and, though this has yet to be proved, the custom of decorating a grave with flowers is known to date back at least to Roman times, when bodies were buried with numerous important possessions that might be useful in the afterlife. Miniature gardens were laid out over burial sites so that the spirit of the newly departed could enjoy their tranquillity once they were at peace, and cut flowers were placed alongside tombs as offerings to the Gods.

The ancient Romans would have considered it disrespectful to both the gods and the soul of the person within the grave to take anything left by the bereaved at the graveside and it is still seen as callous and morally wrong to do so. Since at least the early nineteenth century there has been an added deterrent for any would-be flower snatcher – the superstitious belief that taking flowers from a grave would lead the thief to be the next to be buried.

The belief is especially strong where it relates to the picking of living flowers that are growing naturally on a grave, since these are said to indicate that the person buried within was good. Weeds growing on a grave are said to suggest the opposite, which is why many superstitious people take special care to tend to the graves of their loved ones.

A diluted version of these traditions still survives today and has, in fact, experienced something of a resurgence in the West in recent years, with modern graves being decorated with items of clothing, favourite personal effects of the deceased and plastic flowers. It's a change that has caused consternation among traditionalists within the Christian church, who believe the metaphorical message conveyed by live flowers – that their beauty, like human life, is transient, has been lost.

IT IS BAD FORTUNE TO USE SCISSORS ON NEW YEAR'S DAY

New Year is celebrated at different times and in different ways, with a huge range of customs and rituals. New Year's resolutions, for example, can be traced back to the Romans, who made offerings and sacrifices and were on their best behaviour throughout January in order to win favour with Janus, the god of beginnings, and ensure a lucky year. They gave gifts to each other, a custom which continues in Latin countries, and they believed that the beginning of anything, a journey, a chore and especially a new year, was an omen as to how it would unfold.

One traditional belief that survived well into the Renaissance, and that lasts in a diluted form to this day, held that your actions or circumstances on the first day of the New Year set the tone for the whole of the year ahead. This meant that on 1 January (for countries using the Gregorian calendar) cupboards had to be full, fires must be kept burning and any activity that had symbolic links to loss or misfortune had to be avoided.

One such activity was the use of scissors. In folklore, scissors were imbued with special powers to sever more than just the fabric and paper for which they were designed (*see* Never Give a Knife or Scissors as a Gift). In the Middle Ages they were used as protection against witchcraft and were hidden near a doorway to prevent witches from entering, or secreted beneath a cushion or under a rug to make a witch feel uncomfortable in a room and force her to leave without using her wiles to harm the inhabitants. Their protective powers were thought to be magnified if they were left open in the shape of a cross, adding the divine protection of the crucifix to the strength of the iron or steel and the keenness of the sharpened blades. Using such a powerful instrument on the first day of the year, even for a minor domestic task, was frowned upon as it risked cutting off good fortune for the coming year.

NEVER GIVE A KNIFE OR SCISSORS AS A GIFT

One of the best sources we have of the superstitions and old wives' tales that governed the lives of our distant ancestors is a medieval French manuscript called *Les Évangiles des Quenouilles,* which, in around 1470, recorded on parchment the wisdom of six peasant women. The manuscript is a precious resource for those interested in folklore for two principal reasons: firstly, until this time, knowledge of this kind was passed down orally and rarely documented, which means that many of the beliefs and customs of the Middle Ages have been lost to us. Secondly, because it dates from before the vilification of village wise women as witches, the women whose observations appear in it were free to divulge their ancient lore, charms and cures without fear of persecution. Thus we have a richer, more detailed account of the folklore of the time than we could have hoped for once women like the manuscript's authors were shunned, or worse. In 1507 an English translation of the manuscript, called *The Gospelles of Dystaues,* or *The Distaff Gospels,* was published and within its pages can be found early versions of many of the superstitions we're familiar with today.

Among them is this still commonly held belief that giving a knife or a pair of scissors as a gift will result in the bonds between the giver and the receiver being severed. *The Distaff Gospels* put it like this: 'If a man offers a knife to his mistress as a New Year's gift, you should know that their love will cool off.'

The only antidote to this was for the recipient to give a coin in return. This was seen to count as 'payment' for the knife and ensured that it wasn't technically a gift. All early references to the belief focus on knives, but by the early 1700s the superstition had extended to include scissors, which were also believed to have the power to cut ties between people, their friends and their fortunes. (*See also* It Is Bad Fortune to Use Scissors on New Year's Day.)

ITCHING PALMS

We all like a superstition that presents the possibility that something beneficial might be coming our way and the modern version of this belief allows for a bit of optimism: if your left palm itches, you will soon receive money. Perhaps as a result of our desire for good news, combined with the fact that this is a superstition based simply on an observation rather than an action, it has stood the test of time, though few of us pay much heed to an itch on the right palm, which is said to indicate the imminent loss of a substantial sum.

Some sources suggest that the origin of this belief lies with the Anglo-Saxon practice of rubbing diseased skin with silver to cure it. The first documented use of silver in medicine dates back to the eighth century, when silver filings were used to purify blood and ease heart palpitations and by the twelfth century, the word 'silver' had evolved from the Old English 'seolfor' and it was being used widely for medicinal purposes. Modern scientists now understand the anti-bacterial qualities of the silver ion and it is still used in wound dressings, especially since the rise of antibiotic-resistant infections like MRSA.

However, while we consider an itchy left palm a lucky thing, our Elizabethan forefathers saw it as a curse, linking it to greed and covetousness. Even if the money flowed in, the desire for money, which they believed was indicated by an itching palm, was seen as a very bad quality. In Shakespeare's *Julius Caesar*, Brutus observes: 'Let me tell you Cassius, you yourself are much condemned to have an itching palm.'

While we certainly prize wealth in the modern age, we also recognize the perils of preoccupying greed, and though we don't think of an itching palm as a sign of avarice, we do still say 'he's got itchy palms' of people whom we suspect of trying to swindle money out of us.

LIGHTED CANDLES AND EVIL SPIRITS

Candles have been associated with spiritual activity since pre-Christian times. They were used in pagan ceremonies and the late Egyptians used them in magical rituals in which they stared into the flame before sleep in the hope of seeing the truth in their dreams. By the twelfth century candles had become part of religious tradition and began to appear on church altars and in blessings. Within the Catholic Church they were also used in rituals designed to exorcize demons, and it was this association with the spirit world that gave rise to the belief that a flame would go out in the presence of evil.

A candle spluttering out during a ceremony was said to indicate the presence of a malign spirit, especially on All Hallows Eve, when evil spirits were thought to roam freely. In East Anglia, where Halloween was known as 'Lating Night,' candles were traditionally lit by villagers just before midnight and carried though the fields and common lands. If the flames guttered and the candles died out, evil was afoot; if they went on burning steadily, the villagers could rest in the knowledge that they'd escaped a haunting.

The power of the candle against dark forces was cemented by their inclusion in the list of weaponry prescribed by the Dominican prior and inquisitor Heinrich Kramer, whose treatise on witchcraft and how to repel it became a handbook for the witch-hunters of the Middle Ages.

Later, a candle was customarily placed at the bedside of the sick to keep demons at bay and if it burned blue, it was taken to mean that a ghost had entered the room, perhaps to escort the soul of the dying person to the next realm. If it sputtered out for no apparent reason, it was taken as a sign that the patient was about to pass away. A candle is also often left in a room after someone has died, but this is where European and American folklore diverge. In the US it is considered unlucky to leave a candle burning in a room in which there is no living guardian of the flame, some saying it invites the death of a friend or relative.

BURNING CHEEKS MEAN SOMEONE IS TALKING ABOUT YOU

This superstition is still recited often today if someone feels a burning sensation in either their cheeks or ears. The nature of the words being spoken about you varies in some interpretations: some say a burning on the left side means someone is speaking ill of you, while on the right means you're being praised. In Pennsylvania if both sides burn it's said to mean two people are arguing over you.

All versions have their roots in early superstitions about witchcraft and the ability of wise women to cast spells on people. 'Cheek burning,' as it was known in the Middle Ages, was an indication that some sort of magical influence was at work on the sufferer, so this counter-curse was recited to rebuff the spell:

Right cheek left cheek, why do
you burn?
Cursed be she that doth me any harm:
If she be a maid, let her be staid;
If she be a widow, long let her mourn;
But if it be my own true love – burn,
cheek, burn!

A curse like this would usually have been made only by women, so the final line was included in case the spell had been cast by a witch at the request of the afflicted woman's sweetheart hoping to make her fall more deeply in love with him, in which case she would gladly allow the magic to do its work.

As belief in the power of witchcraft lessened, the phrase was used to refer to people who might be criticizing the sufferer and several less potent antidotes were devised. The Pennsylvanian solution was to bite the corner of your apron, which was said to make back-biters bite their tongues. A more widespread American custom was to lick the tip of your finger and press it on the burning cheek while reciting the names of anyone you suspected; the guilty party was the one whose name was on your lips when you felt your cheek grow cool.

A SUDDEN CHILL THAT CAUSES A SHIVER MEANS SOMEONE HAS STEPPED OVER YOUR GRAVE

We're all familiar with the sensation: you might be merrily chatting away about some inconsequential thing or other when suddenly you shudder, icy fingers creep up your spine and your skin tingles. 'Ooh!' you might exclaim, 'someone's just stepped on my grave.' Few of us actually believe it, but when the phrase was first in use – by at least 1738 when it first appeared in print in Simon Wagstaff's *A Complete Collection of Genteel and Ingenious Conversation* – they really meant it (Wagstaff was one of many aliases of the satirist Jonathan Swift). The saying comes from an earlier legend that the site of your future grave was pre-determined, and that if someone walked over the place where that grave would one day be, you would feel a deathly chill and shiver in response.

This notion relied on the medieval acceptance of fate or destiny. It wasn't until the Renaissance that the concept of individualism began to take root and people started to believe that they could change the course of their lives, who they would become, and where and how they might die.

Most people living in the Middle Ages believed that their life paths were predetermined by God and that their final resting place was therefore set. They also believed that the veil between the living world and the afterlife was thin and porous, allowing spirits, and prophetic sensations, to move freely between the two.

As time went on the phrase spread to America and became established in the legend-rich Appalachian Mountain region. Soon variations began to appear; by the turn of the twentieth century a Welsh version held that the shiver was caused by a donkey walking over the grave, while in Newfoundland it was a goose. This latter version is thought to be an example of a kind of retrospective modification: the shiver induced goose bumps, or gooseflesh, so, gradually, a goose took the place of a person in the phrase. Then, when people began to wonder about the origins of words and phrases, they found themselves asking 'which came first, the goose or the gooseflesh?'

IF A BROKEN CLOCK SUDDENLY CHIMES, THERE WILL BE A DEATH IN THE FAMILY

Many death omens date back to before the scientific revolution of the Renaissance, but this one is comparatively recent. It wasn't until the late sixteenth century that clocks began to appear in people's homes; before then early mechanical clocks were used in church bells (the word 'clock' comes from the French word 'cloche,' meaning bell), which were the only means, aside from the movement of the sun, for people to tell the time. In Tudor times it was only the wealthy who could afford a complex time-piece and for most people, working in the daylight hours and resting at dusk was as accurate as they needed to be with their time-keeping.

Grandfather clocks were becoming popular in the homes of the rich by the middle of the seventeenth century but it wasn't until the mid-eighteenth century that mechanical clocks were a regular feature of ordinary homes. These early clocks needed regular winding to keep time and the winding mechanisms were vulnerable to damage. Over-winding or winding the wrong way could cause the workings of the chime to become unsynchronized or cause the clock to stop completely. To many people, this seemed a sinister sign: having relied for so many generations on the position of the sun to tell the time, the notion that time might stop was alarming. A stopped clock was associated with a life at its end and if one that had long been silent suddenly chimed, it was taken as a message from beyond the grave that a death was imminent.

A book written by the American minister Reverend Samuel Watson in 1873 called *The Clock Struck One, and Christian Spiritualist: Being a Synopsis of the Investigations of Spirit Intercourse by an Episcopal Bishop, Three Ministers, Five Doctors, and Others, at Memphis, Tenn.* illustrates how seriously the superstition was taken. As its curious title suggests, the book is a collection of what we might now call 'paranormal' events, including several accounts of old clocks striking just before a death, including before the deaths of Watson's wife and two of his children.

'It is popular with some people to ridicule facts when they have no evidence of disproving them, or argument to overthrow them,' Watson writes. 'There are many things occurring equally "singular and mysterious" but people do not like to be called "superstitious" and hence rarely mention them.'

WRAPPING A NEWBORN CHILD IN ITS MOTHER'S CLOTHES UNTIL IT HAS BEEN BAPTIZED

While there are still countless superstitious beliefs surrounding childbirth and newborn babies, this one is likely to be less familiar to modern readers. In fact, only just over half of newborns are christened in the UK and America these days, which shows just how much times have changed since this custom was common practice. In the Middle Ages, baptism usually took place within a week of the birth but the many who died before they had been baptized were believed to exist in the 'limbo of infants' – a section of hell set aside for those still sullied by original sin but too young to have committed any personal sins that would consign them to the 'Hell of the Damned.' Similar beliefs existed in European countries; for example, Scandinavian folklore said their souls became will-o'-the-wisps that drifted like mist over marshland.

Between 30 and 50 per cent of medieval babies died in infancy, many in the first days after birth, as a result of infections and diseases that basic medicine could not comprehend and had no means to prevent. This pairing of a high death rate with such fearsome beliefs about where the soul of a lost child would end up fuelled medieval families' faith in superstitious practices that might protect their offspring through this most vulnerable time. The tradition of wrapping a newborn in its mother's clothes was based on the hope that it would be seen by evil spirits that might prey upon it as an extension of her, and be left alone. Other forms of protection included communion wafers and iron amulets placed in the crib and red string tied around the baby's wrist. Knives were also placed in the crib, as the following astonishing rhyme relays:

Let the superstitious wife,
Near the child's heart lay a knife,
Point be up, and haft be down;
While she gossips in the town.
This 'mong other mystic charms
Keeps the sleeping child from harms.

A talisman or mother's clothing also fended off the attention of fairies, who were said to covet the beauty of human babies and to swap them for their own young, which were ugly and deformed. In the days before genetics could explain congenital disorders and birth abnormalities, parents who noticed such variations in their newborns often put them down to this superstition.

WHEN A DOG HOWLS, DEATH IS NEAR

Dogs have been believed to possess a sixth sense for the supernatural since the earliest civilizations and it's possible that this superstition, still widely held today, has its origins in Egyptian mythology. Sirius, the Dog Star, is said to have appeared just before the rising of the Nile and acted as a warning to the people to prepare for a flood, so dogs and gods with the faces of dogs were recognized for their prophetic powers and worshipped from then on.

The Romans also credited canines with an ability to warn of a death and dogs were said to have howled before Caesar's murder and before the death of Emperor Maximinus. These beliefs were carried into the folklore of numerous cultures, where subtle variations can still be found. In Wales there is a legend that says dogs were the only creatures to be able to see the fearsome Hounds of Annwn, while in Irish, Hebrew and Greek tradition their melancholy howl is seen as the first prophetic note of a funeral dirge, which the mourners then imitate in their keening as they follow the funeral procession.

The first direct reference to the superstition in print can be found in the medieval *Distaff Gospels*, which documented the received wisdom of women in the fifteenth century. The 1507 English translation reads: 'What one hereth dogges houle and cry he ought for to stopee his eres, for they brynge euyell [evil] tydynges.'

Over time the prophecies became more precise so that in Europe and Ireland a dog howling relentlessly during the night meant that someone nearby would soon die, while a solitary howl suggested that the hound was marking a death that had just occurred.

The longevity of the superstition owes much to the fact that it inspired numerous pre-eminent authors, who wove it into their work with such dramatic impact that it became firmly entrenched in the public imagination. Shakespeare's *Henry VI* includes the line 'At thy birth, an evil signe . . . Dogs howl'd.' In his poem *Christabel* Samuel Taylor Coleridge describes the howling of a mastiff's bitch and writes: 'some say, she sees my lady's shroud.' In his novel *Martin Chuzzlewit* Charles Dickens describes how 'The howling of a dog before the house, filled him with a terror he could not disguise.'

Modern mediums still credit dogs with the power to sense spirits and to see ghosts that remain invisible to the human eye.

IT IS BAD LUCK TO BURN BEEF BONES

This kitchen superstition comes from an older belief that accidentally burning beef bones was a sign that a great deal of sorrow was coming your way as a result of poverty. The precise origin of the belief is hard to pinpoint accurately but it may stem from the story of St Lawrence, one of the most honoured martyrs of the Roman Church, whose role was to care for the poor and needy. In the year 258 he was told by the Prefect of Rome, who believed the Church had a hidden fortune, to hand over the treasures of that institution. The saint said he would need three days to gather the treasures but instead of bringing gold, he brought all the destitute people of Rome who were being helped by the Church. In his anger the Prefect of Rome ordered that St Lawrence be put to a slow and painful death: he was tied to a grill and slowly burned alive.

An interesting variation of the superstition appears in one of the earliest collections of women's wisdom, the *Distaff Gospels*, published in 1507, and this version provides the link to St Lawrence: 'He that dothe not caste, or suffreth not to caste bones in the fyre shall not haue the toothache for ye honour of saynt Laurens.'

The superstition doesn't appear in print in its modern form until 1840, when it was included in Mother Bunch's *Golden Fortune Teller*, described as an oracle of love, marriage and fate. Mother Bunch adds that 'To burn fish or poultry bones indicates that scandal will be spread about you, and to cast those of pork or veal into the fire inflicts pains in the bones of the person so improvident.'

In addition to honouring the memory of St Lawrence, the everyday homemakers of the medieval and Renaissance periods would have seen burning the bones as unlucky in itself. Most families kept one or two cows at a time and, when slaughtered, the whole of the animal was put to use – the bones were often used for making household utensils like tools, weapons, fasteners and sewing implements.

IF A BAT GETS IN YOUR HAIR YOU ARE POSSESSED BY THE DEVIL

The Roman poet Virgil helped to link the bat to a sense of evil by identifying it with the monstrous winged creatures described in Homer's epic poem *The Iliad*. In the first century AD, charms carved from the bones of bats were used to repel evil, and the Roman naturalist Pliny the Elder recommended fixing the body of a bat upsidedown above a door to ward off misfortune.

In medieval Europe, on the other hand, it was considered bad luck to see a bat in daylight and if one flew into your house it meant a death would soon follow. The animals' nocturnal habits meant that they were considered 'creatures of the night' and thought to associate with witches and the Devil. Some peasants believed that a bat had the power to bewitch you if you got too close and many medieval artistic representations of the Devil depict him with bats' wings. In an age when people believed that God was in a constant state of war with the Devil for their souls, it wasn't unusual for demonic possession to be suspected if someone began to behave strangely. There was no understanding of conditions such as epilepsy or psychosis, and the medieval interpretation of the symptoms of these problems was that the Devil himself had taken over the soul of the sufferer, or that a demon in the form of an animal like a bat had been sent into the body by a witch.

In the eighteenth century, when novels like Bram Stoker's *Dracula* brought the folkloric figure of the vampire to the forefront of public consciousness, public opinion turned against bats even more. While Europeans did everything they could to prevent bats from coming close to them, in China and the Middle East they were welcome visitors. Mythology from both cultures feature bats as symbols of happiness and long-life. Only since hard-fought campaigns by environmentalists has the ecological importance of bats been recognized in the West and they are now a legally protected species.

SAYING 'BLESS YOU' WHEN SOMEONE SNEEZES

This is probably the most common superstition we act upon today. Whether we believe we need to or not, few of us can hear a companion sneeze without saying 'Bless you!' and as well as being the most widely practised superstition in the Western world, it is also one of the oldest. Writing his *Natural History* in 77 AD, the Roman naturalist and philosopher Pliny the Elder asks the question: 'Why is it that we salute a person when he sneezes, an observation which Tiberius Caesar, as they say, the most unsociable of men, as we all know, used to exact, when riding in his chariot even?'

Pliny may not have known the origin of the custom, but an explanation is offered in William Caxton's 1483 manuscript *The Golden Legend, or Lives of the Saints,* which was a translation of one of the most popular religious works of the Middle Ages *Aurea Legenda,* compiled in 1275 by the Italian archbishop and chronicler Jacobus de Voragine. The text describes a pestilence sent to the Christian Romans that was so cruel and sudden that if someone was heard to sneeze, those nearest them said 'God helpe you or Cryst helpe,' knowing that they could be dead within minutes.

Many sources date saying 'Bless you' to the great plague. Although Caxton's reference proves this incorrect (the original text predating the arrival of the bubonic plague by just over a century), it does seem likely that the practice was cemented by the horror of such a virulent and devastating disease from which people could do so little to defend themselves.

At some stage in its history though, the custom of blessing sneezers became linked to the spiritual, rather than the medical dangers of the act. The soul of a person has often been represented by the breath, and it was thought that when someone sneezed, the sudden expulsion of air from their body took their soul with it. In this moment the body of the person was vulnerable to being inhabited by an evil spirit, so the blessing became a form of protection against demonic possession. In Spain when someone sneezes people say 'Jesus!,' because saying the Lord's name offered similar protection.

IF YOU BITE YOUR TONGUE WHILST EATING, IT IS BECAUSE YOU HAVE RECENTLY TOLD A LIE

This belief comes from an earlier superstition that a blister would form on your tongue if you told an outright lie, flattered someone falsely or used clever language to conceal the truth. It was widely believed in from at least the seventeenth century, evidence of which can be found in Shakespeare's *A Winter's Tale,* in which Paulina, knowing she must deliver bad news to the King, speaks the line 'If I prove honey-mouth'd, let my tongue blister.' The medieval notion that the part of the body most directly responsible for a sin would suffer the consequences of its wrongdoing (*see* Never Kill a Robin) was still common in Elizabethan society; thieves often had their right hand cut off as a punishment, and the tongue, in particular, was often described as its own entity where falsehood was concerned. The Bible contains numerous references to support this: Proverbs 26:2 (King James Bible) for example, states: 'A lying tongue hateth those that are afflicted by it; and a flattering mouth worketh ruin.' The widely accepted Christian interpretation was that lies were conceived in the heart under the influence of Satan, so lying of any kind was regarded not simply as an example of a human failing, but as the direct work of the Devil. This was enough to convince most God-fearing people of the need to tell the truth, but the Bible is not the source of this superstition. There is documentary evidence that the threat of a blistered tongue hung over the ancient Greeks as well. In around 275 BC, the Sicilian poet Theocritus included the following reference in his *Idylls*: 'Thee I'le sing, Thee sweet, nor midst my song tell-tale Blisters rise, and gall my Tongue.'

So it seems likely that the idea was adopted into British culture directly from translations of early Greek poetry. Over time the blister became a less specific burning sensation, and the superstition spread to the US. 'The Despot's Song', published anonymously in Baltimore in 1862 by an author opposed to the Union government uses the idea to discredit the then President Abraham Lincoln, to whom he gives the lines:

Lie! Lie! Lie!
As long as lies were of use;
But now lies no longer pay,
I know not where to turn,
For when I the truth would say,
My tongue with lies will burn!

A BRIDE MUST SEW A SWAN'S FEATHER INTO HER HUSBAND'S PILLOW TO ENSURE FIDELITY

Superstitions tend to cluster around the most significant moments in life, which is why there are so many surrounding birth, death and marriage. The start of married life, like the start of the New Year, was said to determine how successful the union would be, so newlyweds traditionally followed all sorts of wedding-day customs designed to ensure a happy life together, many of which continue to this day. There was one superstitious act, though, that the bride carried out in secret: to keep her new husband faithful she would sew the feather of a swan into his pillow.

Placing items inside or under pillows was traditionally seen as a way of influencing a person's behaviour or wellbeing. Anyone afraid of being bewitched would place a knife beneath their pillow to keep witches away and it was thought that sleeping with a careful selected posy of flowers beneath your pillow would allow you to dream of your future spouse. These beliefs mirrored ancient African witchcraft customs, in which 'voodoo' charms like bones, hair, rags or strings placed under a pillow were said to cause sleeplessness or even death through so-called 'Pillow Magic.'

The significance of the swan's feather in ensuring fidelity came from the bird's reputation in folklore for faithful love, founded on the fact that, unlike most other birds and animals, they mate for life. Swans appear in the legends of many cultures; one of the oldest is from India about a nymph, Urvasi, who fell in love with a mortal man, Puruvaras, and pledged to stay with him as long as she never saw him naked. A god, envious of their love, tricked Puruvaras into breaking her condition and Urvasi was forced to flee from him. Loyal Puruvaras searched endlessly for her and finally found her swimming with other nymphs in the guise of swans. Some versions say she refused to return to him, others that he was granted immortality to remain with her forever. Parallel tales can be found in Egyptian and Roman mythology and in legends from Greenland, Eastern Siberia and Ireland, where they were said to be bewitched maidens, or carriers of the souls of women who had died as virgins. Later, portrayals of their devotion in Wagner's operas *Parsifal* and *Lohengrin* and Tchaikovsky's famous ballet *Swan Lake* cemented the swan's image as an emblem of devotion.

PUT A PINPRICK IN EMPTY EGGSHELLS

A reference to this superstition can be found in the Roman philosopher Pliny the Elder's *Natural History,* from the first century AD. 'There is no one . . . who does not dread being spell-bound by means of evil imprecations; and hence the practice, after eating eggs or snails, of immediately breaking the shells, or piercing them with the spoon.'

Although belief in witchcraft reached its height in the sixteenth and seventeenth centuries, women had been being persecuted for practising magic since Roman times, not for their association with the Devil, as was the case in the witch hunts of the Middle Ages, but for practising outside the strict control of the Roman government, which relied on certain kinds of magic but outlawed any that it deemed a threat to its power.

It seems that the Romans believed witches might use intact eggshells to cast spells on the people who'd eaten them, and by 1486 this suspicion had been documented by the Catholic inquisitor Heinrich Kramer in his infamous witch-hunt manual *Malleus Maleficarum* ('Hammer of Witches'):

> ***We have often found that certain people have been visited with epilepsy or the falling sickness by means of eggs which have been buried with dead bodies,***

especially the dead bodies of witches, together with other ceremonies of which we cannot speak, particularly when these eggs have been given to a person either in food or drink.

Others held that a shell could be used in the same way as a voodoo doll to inflict pain on whoever had eaten it by piercing them with pins, but by the late sixteenth century people had begun to speak out against the torture and killing of women accused of witchcraft. Among them was English MP Reginald Scot, who set out to prove that witchcraft did not exist by documenting the methods inquisitors claimed were used by witches and showing that they were simply tricks of the mind. His 1854 book *Discoverie of Witchcraft* mentions the belief that witches would use eggshells as boats and simulate rough seas with them to cause shipwrecks. Despite his efforts to illustrate the fallacy of this accusation, many people continued to believe that shells could be used by witches either to enact storms or to literally carry them out to sea to create havoc in the waves. Piercing a hole in the shell or crushing it completely was the only remedy.

HOLDING YOUR BREATH WHEN PASSING A CEMETERY

Graveyards have been the subject of superstition since burial rites were first performed for the dead. In ancient cultures the rituals surrounding burial grounds were, of course, regarded as dutiful rather than superstitious and this particular belief may have originated from a blending of the practical with the spiritual. Although they had no notion of the way in which infectious disease could be passed through the air, the smell of decomposing bodies made people wary of breathing in the vapours emitted by a corpse, so covering the mouth became customary. On the spiritual level, early man associated the breath with the life force, or soul, as a result of simply observing that the spirit seemed to leave the body with the exhalation of the final breath.

The soul is linked with the breath linguistically too: *pneuma* is an ancient Greek word for breath and is translated in religious contexts as 'spirit' or 'soul.' The English word spirit comes from the Latin word *spiritus,* which means breath, and in Hindu philosophy the word *prana* means breath, but also 'life force.' It stood to reason in their minds that just as the spirit could be exhaled from the body of someone on their deathbed, that soul might then be inhaled into the body of a living person.

Over time, beliefs like these were incorporated into folklore and compounded by stories of ghosts and possession by evil spirits. Graveyards were believed to be full of the spirits of the dead, either returning to communicate with their loved ones or trapped in limbo as a result of their earthly sins. Since it was thought to be more common for the spirits of the sinful to loiter around graveyards (the good spirits being happily ensconced in Heaven), the chances of becoming possessed by an evil soul were greater and certainly worth holding your breath to avoid.

NEVER OPEN AN UMBRELLA INDOORS

This is one of the most commonly recited superstitions of our age and the evidence suggests that it is of comparatively recent origin, as umbrellas weren't widely used until the nineteenth century. Fans of speculation and conjecture might appreciate the following unverified offer of explanation: the earliest umbrellas were used as sunshades rather than to keep the rain off and in ancient Egypt, where such parasols were used for this purpose, ceiling-less temples were constructed for the worship of the sun gods. Some sources have it that raising an umbrella inside such a temple was a direct affront to the gods and a rejection of the sun's blessing, for which there was a hefty price to pay.

As there is no documentary evidence of this belief in the numerous collections of superstitions made in the years between the fall of the ancient civilizations and the nineteenth century, it seems that an alternative explanation is more likely, if less beguiling. One of these is the possibility that the umbrella, along with other upturned items in the home including lucky horseshoes hung in the open-end-up position (*see* Horseshoes), could be used as resting places for mischievous fairies and pixies. Some word-of-mouth reports of this superstition include stories of goblins living in folded umbrellas who might be released into the home if you opened one indoors, and these kinds of superstition were commonly handed down through the generations with small modifications to allow them to fit the living arrangements of the day.

The exact nature of the misfortune due to rain down on you if you do open an umbrella inside varies from era to era and place to place. These days it's mostly just considered 'bad luck,' but in the late 1800s opening one and holding it directly above your head was said to be a sign of a forthcoming death. A version of the superstition that appeared in a compendium of American folklore published two decades ago suggests that by opening an umbrella beneath a roof, the guilty party forfeits the protection that the house has to offer. Most superstitious homeowners took care to ensure that their house was protected from the influence of evil spirits through the placement of a talisman or 'lucky' charm at the entrance, but opening an umbrella within it created a kind of independent realm, existing under its own jurisdiction and lacking the blessings required to keep you safe within it.

FRIDAY 13TH IS AN UNLUCKY DAY

This is another of those bad-luck beliefs that even the most rationally minded among us are still haunted by today. Moving into a new home, starting a new job or getting married on Friday 13th are all considered unlucky and many of us would openly admit to doing our best to avoid them. These days, when we hang onto a belief of this kind, we tend to think of it as being rooted in something so ancient it's not our place to question it. And yet this most deeply engrained superstition can't be found in documentary evidence any earlier than the mid-twentieth century. It seems instead to be a relatively modern combination of two much older beliefs. The first is that Friday is an unlucky day. Records of this can be found in print from the fourteenth century, including in Chaucer's *Canterbury Tales* published around 1390, and all sources are agreed that it stems from the Christian belief that the Crucifixion of Jesus took place on a Friday. Since the early Christian Church, Good Friday has been marked by fasting and prayers in commemoration of Jesus's death and is followed by celebrations of his resurrection on Easter Sunday. Friday has since been regarded as the most unlucky day of the week and it was seen as foolish to start any piece of work, do household chores or set out on a journey on a Friday. (*See* A Bed Changed on Friday Will Bring Bad Dreams.)

The part of the superstition pertaining to the 13th day of the month has a less direct source. It seems to have evolved from a distrust of the number thirteen, which has its roots in the story of the Last Supper (*see* The Number Thirteen). Jesus and his twelve disciples made the number of people dining thirteen, and since Judas Iscariot then betrayed Jesus, this made people distrustful of the number. A separate superstition holds that it's unlucky for thirteen people to sit down to eat, and while this belief has waned, the number thirteen has kept its negative associations in the modern fear of Friday 13th.

NEVER USE A CROSSROADS AS A MEETING PLACE

Much of the superstition that prevailed during the medieval period stemmed from the depth of people's belief in evil spirits. With as much certainty as we know the earth to be round, the people of the Middle Ages believed that their world co-existed with a spirit world from which they were divided by the finest of veils. Anything that represented a boundary was seen as a kind of seam where the two worlds met; one which might part at any moment to let demons, vampires, goblins or ghosts spill through to haunt ordinary folk. Numerous superstitions grew up around crossroads. On the Isle of Man people would take their brooms to the crossroads at nightfall to sweep away evil spirits. In the Böhmerwald Mountains in Germany witches were expelled by cracking whips at a remote crossroads and in Bali ceremonies are held at crossroads to oust devils. In Roman mythology, Hecate, goddess of the night and protector of witches, appeared at crossroads and witches were thought to meet there.

Christian tradition added to these pagan associations when the bodies of people who had committed suicide were buried at crossroads. Until 1823 suicides were not permitted to be buried in either consecrated ground or at unconsecrated public burial sites and it wasn't until 1880 that their burial could be accompanied by prayers. For some years it was customary for burial sites for these bodies to be situated on the outer edges of towns or at crossroads. Gallows were also often erected at crossroads on the edge of towns and this magnified their pre-existing reputation as a place where the damned would congregate. The souls of these 'sinners' were thought to be denied access to heaven as a result of their wrong-doings and people were fearful that they might return to the homes they'd lived in and haunt the inhabitants. A crossroads burial was believed to confuse the soul, consigning it to linger for eternity at the junction between paths.

CROSSED KNIVES AT THE TABLE SIGNIFY A QUARREL

There are lots of superstitions about cutlery; most feature mild-mannered omens covering everything from receiving a visitor to getting married, but things turn darker when the cutlery is crossed. During the English witch hunts of the mid-seventeenth century, East Anglian vicar the Reverend John Gaule published a book titled *Select Cases of Conscience Touching Witches,* in which he describes the laying of a knife across another piece of cutlery as one of the many actions being used to persecute innocent women for the crime of witchcraft: 'Some Marks of witches altogether unwarrantable, as proceeding from Ignorance, humor, superstition . . . are . . . The sticking of knifes acrosse.'

Gaule's book is a fascinating documentation of the various practices associated with witchcraft, but its historical significance came from the influence it had on public opinion, rather than its detailing of witch methodology. Gaule's purpose in recording such 'signs of witchcraft' was to show the cruelty of those who persecuted innocent women for crimes of which they weren't guilty. The infamous Matthew Hopkins, self-styled 'Witchfinder General,' was responsible, along with his associates, for more hangings for witchcraft than had taken place in the previous hundred years, including the deaths of 300 women in the space of two years from 1644 to 1646. Gaule's publication exposed Hopkins's corrupt methods and began a campaign to suppress witch-hunting which resulted in Hopkins having to appear in court to be questioned about his methods. Hopkins retired the following year.

Just over fifty years later the crossing of cutlery was still seen as unsettling, as this extract from an article in *The Spectator* from 1711 illustrates:

> ***The Lady seeing me quitting my knife and fork, and laying them across one another upon my plate, desired me that I would humour her so far as to take them out of that figure, and place them side by side.***

It's still deemed inappropriate to cross cutlery at the end of a meal, though these days it's regarded less of a sign of witchcraft and more as bad table manners and perhaps prophetic of a quarrel with the offended chef.

TO DREAM OF A LIZARD IS A SIGN THAT YOU HAVE A SECRET ENEMY

Many of the superstitions handed down to us through the generations concern prophetic omens of one kind or another. Methods for divining some small clue about the future flourished in the days when most people believed that their life paths were set and their fate pre-determined; dreams were a rich source of material for interpretation.

A Saxon manuscript listing dreams and their meanings, compiled in around 1050, appeared in Oswald Cockaye's *Leechdoms* in 1866 and featured an extensive range of dream subjects with a wide range of interpretations. Dream analysis had a similar level of popularity to other fortune-telling methods such as tarot cards, palmistry and tea-leaf reading, all of which provided a sense that if you couldn't change the future, you could at least be prepared for it. Omens of bad luck or coming strife were particularly important in allowing people to feel that forewarned was forearmed.

In dream analysis, as in much traditional folklore, animals and birds are often linked to human attributes or flaws that seem to be mirrored by their natural behaviour (*see* A Bride Must Sew a Swan's Feather into her Husband's Pillow to Ensure Fidelity). Lizards were associated with trickery and deception because of their ability to camouflage themselves and use tricks to escape capture, such as shedding their tails if caught by a predator. Naturally, lizards feature most prominently in the mythology of countries where they exist in the greatest numbers. In Australia, for example, there are many superstitious beliefs about the carnivorous goanna (including that they snatch small children), which were started by the early European settlers who must have feared them, and are now entrenched in the bushlore of the outback farming community.

In India, where geckos are a common sight both inside and outside the home, the superstitious go into overdrive if a lizard falls from the rafters and lands on you. Enormous significance is placed on the precise part of your body the lizard touches in its descent, with sixty-five different prophetic possibilities to be interpreted depending on the exact bone of your foot or section of your scalp the gecko touches.

While most of the pseudoscience that existed before the Renaissance faded out of favour as more empirical methods for explaining the universe were discovered, sleep is one of the few areas in which modern science is still relatively in the dark. Dream analysis is still popular to this day, with thousands of different books on the subject in print in Europe and America.

A CHILD'S NAILS SHOULDN'T BE CUT BEFORE ITS FIRST BIRTHDAY

The significance of the hair and nails in folklore dates back to early Egypt, when it was believed that a potion made by stirring together hair, nails and human blood could give the mixer complete power over whichever unfortunate soul the samples had come from. The potency of the ingredients came from the fact that they were thought to represent the person on an elemental level.

Hair and nails were certainly used in sixteenth-century spells designed to protect against evil curses. Archaeological evidence of this practice exists in the form of witch bottles – glass bottles into which were placed hair and nail clippings, pins, wine or urine. The idea was that any curse that had been directed at the owner of the witch bottle would be attracted to the hair and nails and trapped inside the bottle, held there by the pins and washed away by the wine or urine. They were common during the mid-sixteenth century and have been discovered hidden beneath the floors and inside chimney breasts of houses from this era.

Experts in Wicca suggest that many of the uses for hair and nails in Western witchcraft have their origins in *The Venidad*, a Zoroastrian book of laws written in the fifth century BC. In these early scriptures the hair and nails are said to be used as instruments of evil by witches and sorcerers (of whom Zoroaster, as the prophet for one of the first monotheistic religions, heartily disapproved) because they grew with a life of their own and could be cut off the body and used in spells.

It is traditional in many cultures for hair and nails to be buried or burned to prevent them from falling into hands that might put them to such uses and this practice continued in Great Britain and Ireland well into the nineteenth century. For infants, who were especially vulnerable to the forces of evil, it was deemed by many parents to be too risky to cut their nails at all until they were over twelve months old.

SPITTING TO WARD OFF EVIL

These days spitting is usually regarded as both unhygienic and uncouth, but spitting hasn't always had such a grimy reputation. In the Gospel of John, Jesus spits on the ground and mixes his saliva with the dirt to make mud, which he applies to the eyes of a blind man and restores his sight. In ancient Greece spitting was a way to counteract the advances of malevolent spirits and in AD 77 Pliny the Elder wrote 'We are in the habit of spitting to repel contagion.'

It does seem to have been viewed as a superstitious act even in those days though, as the ancient Greek philosopher Theophrastus, writing his study of human motivations *The Characters*, includes in his description of 'The Superstitious Man': 'If he sees a maniac or an epileptic man, he will shudder and spit into his bosom.' Maniacs and epileptics were in those days thought to be possessed by demons, and the condition was believed to be catching.

Spitting on to the bosom is a custom that still exists in Greece and Cyprus, although over time it became unnecessary to actually spit to evoke the protection it offered and the sound 'ptew' was used instead. 'Ptew, Ptew mi me matiasis' is still commonly recited in Greece to repel the Evil Eye (*see* The Evil Eye) and can be roughly translated as 'Spit, spit, I spit on myself to protect myself from the Evil Eye.' The most superstitious will still lift the clothing away from their chest at the neck and imitate spitting onto their chest.

Across the world fishermen traditionally spit into their nets to ensure they get a good catch. In the UK and America boxers spit on their knuckles before a fight and pretending to spit on each hand before tackling any difficult task is common in many cultures. The Irish had a custom of spitting on horses to keep them safe from fairies, who were said to be repelled by anything unclean. The fairies were wrong, however, as modern science has discovered that saliva is in fact an excellent antiseptic, so when we say we're 'licking our wounds' we probably really should be.

NEVER CHOOSE A REDHEAD AS A BRIDESMAID AS SHE WILL STEAL THE GROOM

Suspicion and persecution of redheads is not a modern phenomenon restricted to playground bullying. The Middle English poem *Proverbs of Alfred,* thought to have been written in the latter half of the twelfth century, contains the following piece of 'wisdom': 'The rede mon he is a quet [wicked man]; for he wole the thin uvil red [he will give thee evil counsel.]' Red-haired women were viewed with even more misgiving. In Jewish mythology, Lilith (identified in the Old Testament as Lamia, or in some versions simply as 'screech-owl' or some other night bird) is said to be the first wife God created for Adam, who was thrown out of the Garden of Eden because of her refusal to accept Adam's superiority and went on to marry the Devil and have children by him who were part human, part demon. Lilith is always depicted with red hair, such colouring said to indicate fieriness and a desire for sexual dominance.

The same theme is apparent in depictions of Eve following her fall. Michelangelo's *Temptation and Fall,* painted on the ceiling of the Sistine Chapel between 1508 and 1512, shows a brown-haired Eve being offered the apple by Satan (in the guise of a red-haired serpent woman). In the adjacent fresco, in which she is being expelled from the Garden of Eden for biting the forbidden fruit, her hair is painted red.

Eve's red hair is a physical manifestation of her sin and through this association red-haired women have been branded seductresses. The superstition in question suggests that a redhead shouldn't be trusted as a bridesmaid in case she uses her powers of temptation to lead the groom astray. Numerous other superstitious beliefs stemmed from this sexualized reputation, including that red-haired children are the result of their mothers' indelicacy.

Distrust of redheads was exacerbated by their rarity. Only 4 per cent of the world's population have red hair and in many parts of the world it's barely ever seen. Scotland and Ireland have the highest percentage of red-haired citizens, followed by Scandinavian countries. In Denmark it's considered an honour to give birth to a redheaded child, but in Corsica, where the colouring is much less common, it's customary to spit and turn around to avoid bad luck if you pass a redhead on the street.

KEEPING FINGERS CROSSED TO MAKE WISHES COME TRUE

Crossing fingers to make wishes come true is such a commonplace custom that we barely register it as superstitious. Its use is so widely recognized that the phrase 'fingers crossed' peppers our discussions of every aspect of our lives that involve chance, from our most mundane anticipations to our wildest ambitions. However, despite the many records of good-luck customs made from the seventeenth century onwards, there is no mention of crossing the fingers for luck in print until the early twentieth century. Traditionally people seem to have crossed their legs instead. In 1595, the English dramatist George Peele's satirical romance *The Old Wives' Tale* referred to sitting crossed-legged and saying your prayers backwards as a good-luck charm and *A Provincial Glossary of Popular Superstitions* collected by the English lexicographer Francis Grose in 1787 states: 'It is customary for women to offer to sit cross-legged, to procure luck at cards for their friends. Sitting cross-legged, with the fingers interlaced, was anciently esteemed a magical posture.'

It is possible that the interlaced fingers of the cross-legged women provoked the modern finger-crossing custom, although many sources suggest that its origin is Christian rather than pagan. Some theories hold that it is a variation of the subtle sign of the cross that early Christians made to make themselves known to each other when the practice of their religion was a crime. However, the lack of documentary evidence for this suggests it may be another example of a historical explanation being tacked on to a modern custom. More plausible is the possibility that crossed fingers evolved as shorthand for making the sign of the cross over the whole body, by touching the forehead, chest and each shoulder. This gesture was made to cure illness from the eleventh century onwards and as a form of protection against evil from at least the seventh century, as this extract from a 1618 work by English Puritan William Perkins shows: 'The crossing of the body . . . that we may be blessed from the Devil . . . wherein the crosse carrieth the very nature of a Charme, and the use of it in this manner, a practice of Enchantment.'

These days saying the words takes the place of physically crossing the fingers in many cases, although the visual image of crossed fingers is still powerful (in the UK it is the emblem of the National Lottery). Over time the action now has acquired a secondary meaning too; if you tell a lie or make a promise you don't intend to keep, you can cross your fingers behind your back to signify that you don't mean it, which might originally have been a way of evoking the protection of the cross to nullify the sin of lying.

COVERING MIRRORS AFTER A DEATH IN THE HOME

In the superstition-riddled sixteenth century, mirrors were seen as portals into an unnatural, alternative world presided over by the Devil. Anyone showing the sin of vanity by staring for too long at their reflection risked seeing a vision of Satan standing beside them. This was particularly terrifying in times when many people believed their reflection to be an embodiment of their soul (*see* Breaking a Mirror), and while their soul was outside their own body, it was vulnerable to being snatched, either by the Devil himself, or by the departing spirit of the recently deceased.

Their body too, was under threat of possession by another soul while their own was trapped in the looking glass, and it seems that a combination of all these fears fuelled the custom of covering mirrors in a house where someone had died. The earliest known reference in print to the practice comes from the 1780s and it seems to have been prevalent throughout the nineteenth century and was still common in the early 1900s. In his 1911 study of mythology *The Golden Bough,* the Scottish anthropologist, Sir James George Frazer gives the most thorough explanation of the practice to be found in print: 'It is feared that the soul, projected out of the person in the shape of his reflection in the mirror, may be carried off by the ghost of the departed, which is commonly supposed to linger about the house till the burial.'

Other variations on the theme co-existed with this one, including the belief that if you look into a mirror in a room in which someone has recently died, an apparition of the corpse looking over your shoulder will appear in the reflection. This belief is common in Europe and America, where mirrors were used to catch ghosts. An old New Orleans voodoo technique was employed to trick spirits into being captured: a large mirror was placed in a doorway so that the ghost would walk into it thinking it was entering a room. Instead it would be trapped forever behind the glass.

A BED CHANGED ON FRIDAY WILL BRING BAD DREAMS

This old wives' tale is a combination of two superstitious beliefs. The first is that starting any piece of work on a

Friday, including minor household chores, was thought to be a bad omen (*see* Friday 13th Is an Unlucky Day). Friday was the day that biblical sources suggest the crucifixion of Jesus took place and Friday has been set aside as a day of remembrance of Christ's suffering since the days of the early Church. Farmers wouldn't begin a harvest on a Friday, boats wouldn't set sail and anyone who'd recovered from an illness would stay in bed for an extra day rather than get up for the first time on a Friday. In all these cases lives depended on the plentiful supply of good fortune; at sea especially, the smallest piece of bad luck could have catastrophic results and people dealt with the uncertainties ahead by adhering to rituals they believed would protect them. This way of thinking naturally extended into the home and women would never begin a household task on a Friday for fear of bringing misfortune on the whole household.

The particular significance of changing the bed came from the marriage of Friday's bad luck with superstitious beliefs about the influence of a bed on the sleeper's dreams. Today's scientists still struggle to explain many aspects of the way our brains work while we sleep and two hundred years ago it was thought that spirits, both good and evil, could visit people in their dreams. In the 1800s changing the bed on a Friday was said to allow the Devil to take control of a person's dreams for a week, while 'turning the bed' on the wrong day(both Fridays and Sundays appear in the records as inauspicious), could be an omen of a forthcoming death. Turning the bed meant turning the mattress over, a necessary chore in the days when mattresses were stuffed with natural materials such as straw, feathers and animal hair, but turning one on an unlucky day risked 'turning the luck.' Unsettled dreams were also said to be caused by any interruption to the bed making, especially a fit of sneezing, which would lead to fitful sleep.

PUTTING SALT ON THE DOORSTEP OF A NEW HOUSE TO WARD OFF EVIL

Salt has been used as an emblem of purity since Classical times. It was used in religious ceremonies in ancient Greece and Rome and in the holy water used during baptisms in the Catholic Church. As early as 800 BC there are written records of salt being used in this way. Homer's *Iliad,* for example, refers to meat being sprinkled with holy salt to sacrifice to the gods. These ritualistic practices transmuted into superstitions during the Middle Ages, when people sought comfort from the harsh living conditions, poor harvests and epidemics that plagued them, and blamed their hardships on the influence of the Devil.

Putting salt on the doorstep of a new home was just one of the many rituals carried out to cleanse evil from a dwelling place and to bless and protect the new inhabitants. In the Middle Ages, when evil spirits were thought to roam freely in the form of demonic animals, goblins and fairies, the entrance to the home had to be heavily protected to stop them from getting in. Alongside lucky charms and amulets (*see* Horseshoes), salt was sprinkled on the floor and rubbed into the doorstep to repel evil with its cleansing power.

The strength of medieval belief in the efficacy of salt as a charm against evil is illustrated in a 1486 account of a witch trial in the *Malleus Maleficarum* ('Hammer of Witches'), the most influential publication in the witch hunts of the Middle Ages: 'The Judge and all his assessors must . . . always carry about them some salt consecrated on Palm Sunday . . . for the banishing of all power of the Devil.'

This faith in the power of salt to counteract witchcraft persisted well into the nineteenth century. In the English writer William Howitt's *Rural Life in England*, published in 1838, he describes a Nottinghamshire shoemaker who 'had standing regularly by his fireside a sack-bag of salt and of this he frequently took a handful, with a few horsenail stumps, and crooked pins, and casting them into the fire together, prayed to the Lord to torment all Witches and Wizards in the neighbourhood.'

Offering someone salt and helping them to it, though, was deemed very bad luck: 'Help me to salt, help me to sorrow' was recited from early 1800s, and we still throw a pinch of salt over our shoulder to ward off bad luck if we spill some (*see* Spilling Salt).

PLACING SHOES UPON A TABLE WILL BRING BAD LUCK

Common from the late 1800s, this superstition doesn't appear in print before 1869, leading to modern speculation that it may simply have stemmed from the housewife's instinctive reluctance to allow muddy, possibly manure-covered boots on the table on which she'd soon be laying out the supper. This theory is scuppered by the fact that most early nineteenth-century examples of the superstition specify that new shoes are responsible for the direst of consequences.

The repercussions vary from signifying an argument to prophesying a death and many macabre origins are suggested. Some sources hold that it comes from an aversion to anything that reminds people of the gallows, and was based on the unfounded notion that prisoners were hanged with their shoes on and that once the noose had done its job and was slackened, the tips of their toes would tap on the platform. Others attribute it to the tradition of dressing a corpse in new clothes for the wake, when the body would be laid on a table in the family home until the time of the burial. It is also ascribed in some quarters to the tradition in mining communities of breaking the news of the death of a miner to his family by placing his boots on the table.

Appealing as each of these explanations may be, there is little evidence to support any of them, yet the absence of a plausible source has done nothing to diminish the power of the superstition. In his 1932 collection of folklore *Those Superstitions,* Sir Charles Igglesden includes a tale about the Duke of Wellington Arthur Wellesley, twice British Prime Minister and fearless victor of the Battle of Waterloo who 'instantly discharged an old servant because he placed his Grace's boots on a table.'

Anyone sharing the Duke's aversion could counteract the curse by spitting on the soles of the shoes (*see* Spitting to Ward off Evil) or by ensuring that the person who put them there is the one to remove them.

NEVER TAKE A BROOM WITH YOU WHEN YOU MOVE HOUSE

While most household items have some superstition or other attached to them, those surrounding brooms are stuck to with extra tenacity by the superstitious because of their long association with witchcraft. According to folklore prevalent across Europe, witches used broomsticks to fly to their magic meetings, called sabbats, which resulted in the belief that the broomstick was particularly receptive to the influence of spirits and spells.

Originally brooms were used for pagan fertility magic because of their phallic shape. They were taken into the fields and mounted by farmers who would leap high in the air on them in the hope that their crops would grow to great heights. This early association with magical power meant that they were soon put to use for other household spells: they were thought to be able to repel black magic if they were placed across the threshold of a home and were used as wands for charms and cures by rural wise women. In the Czech Republic a festival called Čarodějnice (the burning of the witches) still takes place on 30 April each year, when it's traditional for people to burn broomsticks on large communal bonfires.

Many modern Wiccans follow the traditions of their medieval predecessors in using a broom as an altar tool during rituals. They are used for clearing a sacred space by sweeping away negative or distracting energy and it is this association with spiritually cleansing a room that gave rise to this particular superstition. A new broom was said to bring good luck to a new home, while using an old broom in a new house risked bringing evil spirits from the old dwelling into the new one. A German tradition for healing a house after misfortune has befallen someone in the household was for everyone to take a broom and sweep from the centre of the house outwards until the negative energy had been banished.

Another strongly held superstition about brooms is that it's unlucky to buy one in May: 'Brooms bought in May, sweep the family away.' It is also said to be unlucky to sweep after dark, a belief which comes from the fourteenth-century persecution of witches, when a woman seen wielding a broom after dark was suspected of sweeping a spell towards someone and could be tried and burned for witchcraft.

NEVER LEAVE A ROCKING CHAIR ROCKING WHEN EMPTY

Rocking chairs didn't appear in England until 1725, but since this time they have been linked to the two groups of people most often associated with the spirit world: the very elderly and witches. Faith in the close connection between the living and the dead was strong in the eighteenth century and many people believed in ghosts. The souls of the dead were thought to pay regular visits to the homes they had left behind, sightings of apparitions on staircases would often be reported (*see* It is Bad Luck to Pass Anyone on the Staircase) and in the rocking chairs the recently deceased had favoured towards the end of their lives. The independent rocking of a chair was taken as a sign that the chair itself was haunted and they often appear in ghost stories creaking away on their own.

The connection with witches evolved from earlier folklore about witches flying on their chairs. Along with the rabid witch-hunt manuals of the Middle Ages that purported to list the signs by which someone could be judged a witch, there were other voices exploring the phenomenon of witchcraft. Not all the women in the docks at witch trials denied the charges levied at them. Some were defiant about the charms and spells they used and fuelled anti-witch hysteria by confirming that they could indeed transform themselves into animals or fly through the air. This resulted in some attempts to understand what these women were experiencing by investigating the potions and brews they cooked up. In *De Praestigiis Daemonum (On the Illusions of the Demons and on Spells and Poisons)* published in 1563, the Dutch physician and occultist, Johann Weyer, found that henbane, deadly nightshade and mandrake were the main ingredients. A potion of these ingredients when rubbed into the skin of the upper thighs and genitals could produce the sensation of flying in the mind of the person anointed with it. This mixture was also applied to broomsticks and to chairs, in the belief that they could be used as vehicles for flight.

By the end of the eighteenth century there are printed records of a superstition that it is unlucky to seat yourself next to an empty chair, since either the spirits of the dead or witches might be sitting there invisibly. Later, the rhythmic movement of an empty rocking chair was thought to provide extra encouragement to such spirits to make themselves at home.

A LOAF OF BREAD TURNED UPSIDE DOWN AFTER SLICING IS PERILOUS

Bread is one of the most important foods in the history of humankind and has been revered since the growing of crops for harvest first began in Neolithic times. Wheat and bread appear in the Old Testament as emblems of the earth's fertility and in the New Testament bread becomes the ultimate gift from God to mankind: 'Jesus took bread, and blessed it, and brake it, and gave it to the disciples, and said, Take, eat; this is my body. (Matthew 26:26, King James).' Christians have made the sign of the cross over new loaves of bread for centuries and since the thirteenth century bakers would often mark the top of loaves with a cross, so turning one upside down would have been seen as sacrilegious.

Bread was sacred to the ancient Greeks and Romans too; Hestia, the Greek goddess of the hearth, domesticity and the family and Vesta the Roman equivalent, were patrons of bread-making and traditionally received the first sacrificial offering in the household. One theory about the origin of this superstition is that turning a loaf upside down was an insult to the goddess of the hearth and offending her put the sustenance of the family at risk. In

England, the consequences of turning a loaf upside down once cut was that the – literal – breadwinner of the family would fall ill, which seems to boost the hearth-goddess notion. Although sources suggest that cutting off the first slice released tempting aromas that would drift down to hell and attract evil spirits, if the loaf was then upturned there is little to support either theory in print.

An alternative explanation comes from eighteenth-century France where each town had a public executioner whose life was loaded with superstition: his house was marked with red paint, he sat in his own pew in church and his family were isolated from the community. It was held to be unlucky to speak to him or touch anything that belonged to him, especially his bread, so much so that the local bakers would bake the executioner's loaf separately and turn it upside down to make sure no one else took it by mistake. In many parts of rural France it is still considered improper to serve or even store a loaf the wrong way up.

IT IS BAD LUCK TO MEET A FUNERAL PROCESSION HEAD ON

No one likes to be reminded of their own mortality, so it is of little wonder that coming face to face with a funeral procession is considered bad luck. In the 1700s the consequences were much worse than a few moments of existential angst. Usually coming across someone else's funeral unexpectedly meant that your own, or at least, that of a member of your close family, wouldn't be long in coming. This belief may have come about in part as a result of the limited understanding people had, pre-scientific revolution, of the diseases that swept through the population. In the days before vaccination, antibiotics or proper hygiene there was a high chance that if someone died from a contagious illness, or from a water-borne disease, others living in close proximity would soon suffer the same fate. With no proper insight into how germs spread people naturally devised their own superstitious explanations.

Among these was that when someone died, evil spirits would cluster round their body, looking for opportunities either to take that body over or to coax the spirit of the recently deceased to join them in their haunting. This led to countless superstitions about the period immediately after death, which in those days was in the hands of the family of the deceased. The body would be kept at home, usually on display for friends and neighbours to come and view, and the rules governing what happened in this time covered everything from the direction the body was carried, to the order the pall bearers walked in to collect it. Anyone meeting the procession on its way to the church could anger these spirits, so to appease them and avoid being the next in the ground, the best advice was to walk along with the mourners for a time and thus transform your 'meeting' into a 'joining.'

In 1787, the English lexicographer Francis Grose included an alternative antidote in his *Provincial Glossary*: 'If you meet a funeral procession, or one passes by you, always take off your hat: this keeps all evil spirits attending the body in good humour.'

From the eighteenth century onwards, pointing at a funeral procession was considered an absolute folly and was said to cause you to die within the month. Pregnant women and newborn children were also warned against accompanying funeral processions, for fear that infants and foetuses were especially tempting prey for the spirits that gathered at an open grave. Since the replacement of the walking funeral procession with the hearse, these old superstitions have fallen out of general use, although older people still often bow their heads for a moment if they notice a coffin being driven by.

COVERING THE MOUTH WHEN YAWNING

The act of covering the mouth when yawning began more than 2000 years ago as result of two distinct theories. The first, incredibly for its time, was that fatal diseases might be passed on in a yawn. Writing in 1499, the Italian historian Polydore Vergil notes in his *De Rerum Inventoribus*: 'Crossynge of our mouth. Alike deadly plage was sometime in yawning, wherefore menne used to fence themselves with the signe of ye crosse . . . which costome we reteyne styl at this day.'

The other reason was equally concerned with wellbeing but more that of the yawner than the wider public, since the ancient Greeks and the classical Maya believed that spirits could enter or leave the body during a yawn. One notion held that the yawn was caused by the Devil himself, to allow demons to enter bodies while the yawner's mouth was stretched wide. Another theory was that the soul of whoever was yawning might fly out of their body and that covering the mouth was the only way to stop it escaping. (*See* Saying 'Bless You' When Someone Sneezes.)

These ideas seemed to be supported by observations physicians made of newborn babies, who often yawn instinctively to fill their newly inflating lungs. Figures on infant mortality in antiquity are hard to pin down precisely, but although rates are thought to have been much lower than in the Middle Ages (estimated at 50–200 deaths per thousand births) there was little understanding of what caused infants to die. In their efforts to document the behaviour of newborns who didn't survive, doctors noted that they often yawned excessively, which seemed to some to corroborate the theory that their souls had escaped through their mouths. To guard against this, new mothers were advised to keep their babies close and use their own hand to cover its mouth whenever it yawned.

By the seventeenth century such superstitious beliefs had combined with a sense that yawning was rude, which meant that people were keener to conceal it. In 1663 the English Jesuit and translator Francis Hawkins advised that 'In yawning howl not, and thou shouldst abstain as much as thou can to yawn, especially when thou speakest.'

There are now several scientific theories about why we yawn, primarily that when tired or bored our breaths become shallow and yawning increases the amount of oxygen entering the lungs. However, nobody really knows exactly why, so perhaps this is one superstition that it is wise to uphold.

KNOCK ON WOOD / TOUCH WOOD

Knocking on wood or saying the words 'Touch wood' to prevent bad luck or stop our hopes from being dashed is thought to stem from an ancient pagan belief in wood sprites called dryads, or tree spirits, who were said to live in the trees, especially oak trees. The Druids believed these spirits were practised in the art of divination and could be called on for protection against evil spirits. This in turn has been suggested by some sources to stem from an even earlier custom prevalent in ancient Greece of calling on the protection of Zeus by touching an oak tree.

These beliefs slotted well into the slew of superstitions by which our more recent ancestors swore. As in rural areas where so much of our folklore was passed on from one generation to the next, there was an inherent faith in the protection the natural world could provide if it was sought in the right way. Touching or knocking on wood were used, as they continue to be today, when discussing an aim or aspiration. This ritual helped people brought up on proverbial warnings against taking things for granted ('Don't count your chickens before they've hatched,' etc.) to talk about their plans without feeling that expressing their wish would cause its failure.

Some sources reject claims of these spiritual origins, however, suggesting instead that, since the earliest records in print of the belief don't appear until the nineteenth century, it may instead come from a children's playground game of chase known as 'tig,' in which touching wood made you immune from being caught. Wherever in our history it came from, however, the custom is still going strong today. In modern times, however, we knock on wood more to preserve our self-esteem in case our scheme should fail than because we fear that mentioning our dreams will scupper their chances of success.

TYING A KNOT IN A HANDKERCHIEF

Most people are familiar with the concept of tying a knot to help us remember something, but an earlier superstition held that a knotted handkerchief could actually work as a charm and protect whoever carried it from evil influences. This belief has been around since at least the fourteenth century and comes from the idea that devils and demons would be drawn to the cunning complexity of a knot, and become so distracted by trying to untie it that they would forget about whatever evil they'd been planning to inflict.

Similar methods are said to have been employed against vampires, including throwing a fishing net, traditionally made from knotted twine, over a vampire's grave. This was said to keep the vampire in his grave, not by trapping him, but by delaying him with the distraction of having to untie so many knots that the sun would rise and banish him back into the earth before he had a chance to attack.

But knots were also used by those feared for their ability to summon evil. Pliny the Elder's *Natural History* refers to knots as cures for fever and also mentions that they were distrusted as a device used by witches although knots are known to have featured in numerous witches' spells. Witches' ladders, for example, were pieces of string or rope made from natural fibres like cotton, hemp or human hair into which between three and forty knots were tied, sometimes accompanied by feathers or other trinkets. In the practice of black magic, witches could use these knotted strings to cast 'death spells', or to inflict pain or loss on another person.

The Scottish clergyman Richard Bannatyne's journal, *Memorials of Transactions in Scotland from 1569 to 1573*, describes the burning of a woman suspected of witchcraft at St Andrews. The author details how in the struggle to tie the woman's hands, her clothes were lifted up revealing a white cloth with strings tied in knots. To her dismay this was taken from her and she cried out: 'Now I have no hoip [hope] of my self.' This was taken as proof of her involvement in witchcraft, but as with so many of the accusations made against witches, this one could equally well have signified that she was using the charms against witchcraft passed on to her through the generations. Many of the superstitions we hold on to today originate from charms against black magic and yet, ironically, many others are simply modernized versions of the spells used by the very women who were accused of witchcraft or even considered themselves practitioners of magic.

LIGHTNING WILL NEVER STRIKE A HOUSE WITH A BURNING FIRE

As one of the most dramatic examples of the irrepressible power of nature, lightning features in the folklore of many cultures. In ancient Rome lightning bolts were the javelins of Jove, the king of the gods, who sent his eagle carrying fiery bolts to punish sinners and to smite whole armies of men. Thunderbirds appear in native American and African legends too. In South Africa a thunderbird known as the *Umpundulo* was thought to peel the bark from trees with his blazing talons; its bright feathers were said to send out lightning and the thunder was caused by the beating of its heavy wings.

Elsewhere, early folklore about lightning was influenced by Old Testament accounts of a wrathful God using lightning against the Philistines, such as these lines from the second book of Samuel: 'And he sent out arrows, and scattered them; lightning, and discomfited them.' (2 Samuel 22:15, King James)

A Yorkshire proverb from the 1870s shows how the biblical became proverbial: 'When tunner's loud crack shaks t'Heavenly vau'ts, It's the Lord wo is callin' ti men o' their fau'ts.'

Fear of evoking God's anger with their flaws resulted in a number of superstitions designed to appease him when storms threatened. Fire is symbolic of faith in many religions, and keeping a fire burning in the hearth was said to protect a home from lightning because it showed that the household was keeping its faith alive. Talking about the storm was avoided as a mark of respect and pointing to it was strictly forbidden, as this extract from an 1862 edition of history magazine *Notes and Queries* illustrates: 'It is wicked to point towards the part of the heavens from which lightning is expected. I have seen a little boy, for this offence, made to kneel blindfold on the floor, to teach him how he would feel if the lightning came and blinded him.'

This interpretation of thunder as a punishment from God has endured among believers well into our more secular age. When a fire destroyed one of the UK's finest cathedrals at York Minster in 1985 and the Bishop announced the news that a lightning strike was to blame, a reader of *The Times* newspaper wrote in to say '"Just lightning" says the Bishop dismissively. To those of us as old-fashioned as I, lightning is the wrath of God.'

NEVER LIGHT THREE CIGARETTES WITH ONE MATCH

This superstition is still widely held today and for some it's as much a part of the ritual of smoking as tapping the end of the cigarette or turning one upside down in a new pack. Most collections of superstitions place its roots in the trenches of the Boer War, when, the theory goes, the expert snipers in the Boer army would spot a flame across the veldt as the first cigarette was lit, take aim as it reached the second and shoot as the third light was being offered, killing the last soldier before he'd had chance to take a single puff.

Historically, superstitions have always engrained themselves most deeply in times of peril. Faced with the very real prospect that life could be snuffed out at any moment, people naturally seek an escape route, and if none is available, they create a battery of superstitious rituals to trick the mind into feeling that they are doing something to protect themselves and help quell the rising panic. It is easy to imagine then that this superstition might have flourished in trench warfare, but there is evidence to suggest that it might have begun with a different army. A reluctance to light three articles with the same match had also been noted among Russian prisoners in the Crimean War, which predated the Boer war by half a century. The reason said to have been given by these prisoners was that rules of the Russian Orthodox Church stated that the only person allowed to light the three altar candles with a single taper was the priest, so no one outside the church would dare to re-enact such a holy rite.

This religious source is supported by the first appearance of the superstition in print. In the 1916 novel *The Wonderful Year* by William Locke, a character named Fortinbras lights the cigarettes of his two companions and uses another for his own:

> *'A superstition,' said he, by way of apology. 'It arises out of the Russian funeral ritual in which the three altar candles are lit by the same taper. To apply the same method of illumination to three worldly things like cigars or cigarettes is regarded as an act of impiety and hence as unlucky.'*

The shrewd salesmanship of Swedish tycoon Ivar

Kreugar, whose match-making empire dominated post-war production of matches, also helped to cement the belief in the public consciousness. The financier and businessman, who was found after his suicide to have committed high-level fraud, is thought to have used his international marketing knowhow to help propagate the myth in order to increase demand for his product and fuelled the fire of this superstition still further.

WEAR A TOAD AROUND THE NECK TO WARD OFF THE PLAGUE

Thankfully the need for protection against the Black Death waned so long ago that superstitions like this one have been consigned to the history books. The mascots and charms that many of us still carry around have their roots in a time when people didn't just use them for good luck, but because they hoped they might save their lives. It is a challenge in the modern age to imagine what life must have been like during the great plagues of medieval and Renaissance Europe. Overcrowding, extreme poverty and the lack of clean water or proper sanitation systems meant that life was precarious even before the arrival of a deadly epidemic. Once the bubonic plague arrived, carried by rats and passed to humans via flea bites, it swept through entire populations, killing 70 per cent of its victims within two to seven days.

The Great Plague of London, which struck in 1665, killed between 75,000 and 100,000 people, representing almost a quarter of the city's population. It was the last in a string of plague epidemics that began in 1499 so people knew all about the horrors that lay ahead. In their desperation to avoid contagion, most who could afford to fled the city, leaving the poor in the decrepit, rat-infested slums that were the hotbed of the disease. Those left behind leapt on anything that offered the chance of protection; as journalist Daniel Defoe describes in his 1722 fiction *A Journal of the Plague Year* there was a craze for 'charms, philtres, exorcisms, amulets, and I know not what preparations against the plague; as if the plague was not the hand of God, but a kind of possession of an evil spirit, and that it was to be kept off with crossings, signs of the zodiac, papers tied up with so many knots, and certain words or figures written on them, as particularly the word Abracadabra, formed in a triangle or pyramid.'

Other methods documented at the time included painting a red cross on the door of infected houses with the words 'Lord have mercy upon us'; the application of a recently killed pigeon to the buboes (grossly enlarged lymphatic glands) or the tying of a frog around the neck to draw out the disease.

Defoe's words sum up the futility of their efforts: 'The poor people found the insufficiency of those things, and how many of them were afterwards carried away in the dead carts and thrown into the common graves of every parish with these hellish charms and trumpery hanging about their necks.'

NEVER BRING LILIES INDOORS

Flowers have been imbued with historical and religious significance for thousands of years and the lily appears in folklore dating back to antiquity. According to Greek legend the flower was formed from drops of the Goddess Hera's spilt breast milk and was a symbol of purity and fecundity. Lilies were woven together with ears of wheat to form crowns worn by brides at marriage ceremonies where they represented their innocence and blessed their fertility. In Roman tradition, lilies were presented to young women by their suitors during the celebration of the spring solstice, and Slavic pagan mythology also has the lily as a symbol of fertility and new life where they were ritually given as gifts at the spring celebration of Ostara, the time of renewal, which eventually became the Christian Easter.

According to Christian legend, lilies sprang from Eve's tears when she and Adam were banished from the garden of Eden. Borrowing from the earlier mythology linking the lily to motherhood and purity, they are also associated with the Virgin Mary and are said to represent her tears. Early paintings depicting the annunciation show the Archangel Gabriel handing Mary lilies as he tells her she is expecting the son of God, and St Thomas was said to have found lilies in place of Mary's body in her tomb after she ascended to heaven. The flower was also said to have sprung from drops of Jesus's sweat in the Garden of Gethsemane the night before the crucifixion, which made them symbolic of the Resurrection. Lilies can often still be seen decorating churches at Easter.

At Roman burials a lily was placed in the hands of the deceased to signify rebirth. This tradition was adopted by the early Church, which eventually appropriated the flower as a Christian symbol of death, and it is from this that the superstition about them bringing bad luck if brought into the home derives.

IT IS UNLUCKY TO DENY A PREGNANT WOMAN HER CRAVINGS

Many readers might view this one as less of a superstition and more of a self-defence measure, since hell is widely known to have no fury like a pregnant woman denied the midnight snack her heart desires. However, this superstition began with the belief that if a woman was made to go without the food she craved, her baby might be 'marked.'

The 1507 translation of medieval manuscript the *Distaff Gospels* includes the opinions of two wise women on this subject: 'I tell you also that when you are with a married woman who could have children or who is pregnant . . . God and reason forbid talking about any food which could not be found at that time if needed, in order that her baby does not have a mark on the body.' A second testimony to this superstition comes from Lady Abonde du Four who claims that if cherries, strawberries or red wine are thrown in the face of a pregnant woman, the child will have marks on the body.

This latter view reflects medieval beliefs in 'Maternal Impression' where experiences the mother has during pregnancy were thought to be visible on the child after its birth. Some American folklore suggests that birthmarks could be found on parts of the body that suffered injuries in a past life, while Iranian mythology states that a mark can appear on an unborn child when its mother touches a part of her own body during a solar eclipse.

However, the unsatisfied cravings theory was most widely believed to be the cause and the naming of birthmarks in several languages reflects this. In Italian they're called *'voglie'*, in Spanish they are known as *'antojos'* and in Arabic *'wiham'*, all of which can be roughly translated as 'wishes', since they symbolized the unfulfilled wishes of the child's mother as she carried the unborn child.

NEVER CUT AN ELDER TREE

The elder tree is revered in pagan folklore for its magical powers and its ability to ward off evil. As a symbol of the natural cycle of life, death and rebirth, its blossom was worn at the May fire festival of Beltane and its branches were used for blessings. It was also an important source of herbal medicine, and its flowers, bark and berries were all used in restorative remedies. Countryside tradition held that it was unlucky to cut down an elder, perhaps because of the early European folktale that it was home to a tree spirit, or dryad called Hylde-moer, who would haunt anyone who chopped the tree down. People were particularly careful to avoid using it to make cradles, as one legend said that Hylde-moer would visit any child laid in a cradle made from her wood and pinch it black and blue. Branches of elder, though, were often cut down and hung over doorways to keep evil spirits at bay and it is only according to Christian legend that bringing elder inside is unlucky.

Christian distrust of Druid customs may have fuelled fear of the elder and during the Middle Ages it was viewed with suspicion by many because of its association with magic and witchcraft. As well as its use in medicine it was also used to make witches' wands. It was said to be the tree that Judas hanged himself from and was sometimes referred to as the 'Death Tree' because its earlier associations with rebirth meant that it was often used at funerals. (*See* Never Bring Lilies Indoors.) It was also thought unlucky to smell the tree or to sleep beneath one.

ALWAYS STIR CHRISTMAS CAKE CLOCKWISE

Fruit cake has been central to Christmas tradition for centuries; its first incarnation was as a plum porridge eaten on Christmas Eve in preparation for a day of fasting on Christmas Day. Over time wheat flour replaced the oatmeal of the original recipe and butter, sugar and eggs were added, as were endless rituals surrounding its preparation. Stirring was a crucial aspect and everyone in the household had to have a turn, even small babies would have their hands held to the spoon to guarantee good luck, and all the stirring had to be clockwise. This rule has nothing to do with the Christian celebration of Christmas; rather, it has its roots in a mistrust of anything moving in an anti-clockwise direction inherited from ancient sun worshipping religions.

Stirring anticlockwise or 'widdershins' as it was called, was said to go against nature because it was against the direction of the sun as it moved through the sky. The significance of the sun and its trajectory was enormous in early religion and many remnants of sun-worship remained in the countryside lore by which many people lived, even long after Christianity replaced paganism as the dominant belief system.

Some of the mistrust of moving in a circle 'widdershins' came from the fact that it was said to be used in witchcraft to summon the Devil and to set spells and curses in motion. A Yorkshire legend states that dancing 'widdershins' nine times around a ring of toadstools would put your life in the hands of the fairies. There were Christian reasons to fear it too, however, given that it might attract the attention of the Devil and it was considered an omen of death to walk 'widdershins' round a churchyard on the way to a funeral.

Many traditions of Christmas cake-making remain even now, though these days we tend to eat it throughout the holiday period, including on the fasting-turned-gorging festival that is Christmas Day.

TOUCHING A CORPSE FOR GOOD LUCK

The modern world has become so distanced from death in the present age that it is hard to imagine feeling an urge to touch a corpse, except perhaps that of a loved one in the moments just after death. Funeral homes and mortuaries are a recent development in human history and for thousands of years the bodies of the recently deceased were kept at home until the time of their burial. During this time it was customary for friends and more distant family members to 'view the body', and while they viewed it they often touched it too.

This practice came from a belief that, as an embodiment of the transition from the world of the living to that of the dead, the corpse possessed supernatural powers that could be harnessed by touching it. A touch to the forehead was said to release people from the fear of death and also ensured that you wouldn't be haunted by the ghost of the deceased. Touching the hand was said to cure warts by passing the essence of the wart to the body, which would cause the warts to shrivel as the body decayed. Other ailments such as goitres, tumours and haemorrhoids were treated with an application of perspiration from a new corpse.

Seventeenth-century records also suggest an even more macabre belief in the power of the dead body; it was said that if the nose of the corpse began to bleed, it meant its murderer was present in the room, and if a suspected murderer was brought to touch the corpse of someone he was accused of killing, it would begin to bleed again to confirm his guilt.

Those wishing to glean good luck from touching a corpse did have to be wary of making an unpleasant discovery though; other superstitions said that if a corpse stayed warm for an unusually long time, or if rigor mortis didn't seem to set in, another death would soon follow.

IF A TOAD OR FROG ENTERS THE HOUSE IT WILL BRING BAD LUCK

This superstition comes from the seventeenth and eighteenth centuries, when toads and frogs were thought to be the familiars of witches. Originally the sight of either creature inside the house was taken as a sign that an enemy was trying to hurt you. If someone who wished you ill fortune had been to a witch to ask her to place a hex on you, it was believed that that witch could inflict pain or suffering by sending their representatives into the households of those to whom they intended harm.

Dorset historian George Roberts wrote in an 1834 account: 'Toads that gained access to a house were ejected with the greatest care and no injury was offered, because these were regarded, as being used as familiars by witches, with veneration or awe.'

Toads and frogs were commonly held to be used in this way and were said to be suckled by the witch from a wart-like 'witch mark.' Witches were also said to be able to take the shape of animals in order to move around unnoticed, and frogs and toads were sometimes suspected of being witches in amphibian form. All sorts of ailments, from muscle weakness to toothache – which it was believed could be as a result of spells being put on the victims – were explained by the presence of a frog or toad in the house. Remedies to help counteract their evil influence varied and there was much contradictory advice in circulation in the 1800s about what action to take if you found one. Some said that simply getting them beyond the boundaries of the home was adequate protection, while others said that if you killed a trespassing frog or toad you would defeat your human enemies and render them powerless to try to harm you again.

PEOPLE WHO LIVE NEAR THE COAST CAN'T DIE UNTIL THE TIDE IS EBBING

The power of the moon over life on earth has been recognized, if not understood, for millennia. The observation that death seemed to be linked to the ebbing of the tide can be found recorded as early as AD 77 in Pliny the Elder's *Natural History*, which notes: 'Aristotle adds, that no animal dies except when the tide is ebbing . . . The observation has been often made on the ocean of Gaul; but it has only been found true with respect to man.'

The moon was thought to exert an influence on all fluids on earth, from the oceans to the fluids within the human body, especially those linked to life and death. The female reproductive cycle is known to be responsive to the moon's phases and more births are said to occur in coastal regions when the tide is in. Spanish coastal areas shared this belief, although those suffering from chronic disease were said to let go of life at the moment when the tide turned.

In *The Golden Bough,* Sir James George Frazer recorded that the belief prevailed both on the Pacific coast of America and in Southern Chile: 'A Chilote Indian in the last stage of consumption, after preparing to die like a good Catholic, was heard to ask how the tide was running. When his sister told him that it was still coming in, he smiled and said that he had yet a little while to live. It was his firm conviction that with the ebbing tide his soul would pass into the ocean of eternity.'

In the UK the superstition was perpetuated by its inclusion in Charles Dickens's novel *David Copperfield,* in which Mr Peggotty observes that people can't die along the coast, 'except when the tide's pretty nigh out . . . If he lives till it turns, he'll hold his own till past the flood and go out with the next tide.'

ACCIDENTS HAPPEN IN THREES

Another superstition still held by many people today, this is one of the particular brand of beliefs in which the perceived antidote often does more damage than good. Popular from the mid-nineteenth century onwards, it may be linked to a similar notion that deaths come in threes, although it is the explanation of simple accidents that results in the most broken crockery. For at least fifty years the superstition had such a strong hold that if someone dropped or broke anything valuable, they would often deliberately smash another two items of lesser value with the aim of 'seeing out' the curse on dispensable items rather than waiting for the next two accidents to creep up on them unexpectedly.

A less destructive way to beat the jinx, common towards

the end of the nineteenth century, was to break a match if two accidents had already occurred, but these days it is not so simple. Over time this belief has expanded its negative influence to become 'bad things come in threes,' which may be a blending of the accidents with the deaths mentioned above. With such a wide range of misfortunes possibly heading our way there is little we can do except brace ourselves for the worst and take solace in the knowledge that at least we saw it coming.

Thankfully another linked idea allows for a degree of optimism: the belief that the third time for anything is lucky. This is thought to have much older origins and can be traced to at least the fourteenth century, when it appears in the Middle English romance poem *Sir Gawain and the Green Knight* with the lines: 'With thee when I return hither; for I have tried thee twice, and faithful I find thee; now, third time, best time.'

CUTTING A LONE HAWTHORN BUSH WILL BRING DEATH

In his *Natural Histories* Pliny the Elder recorded that harming a thorn bush would result in thunderbolts being hurled down onto the spot. To the ancient Romans lightning represented the wrath of Jove, which is an indicator of the seriousness of the crime. Hawthorn was sacred to the Romans: its branches were used as torches at marriage ceremonies and hawthorn leaves were tied to babies' cradles to protect them from evil. As with many plants popular in pagan mythology, the Christian Church turned people against the hawthorn. (*See also* Never Cut an Elder Tree.) At the crucifixion, Jesus's crown of thorns was said to have been made from twisted hawthorn, so it was seen as an omen of death to bring its flowers into the house. The tree was later said to be used by witches to inflict pain on the subjects of their spells.

In 1792 *The Old Statistical Account of Scotland*, which aimed to give details of the people, economy and geography of the country included the following explanatory entry:

There is a quick thorn, of a very antique appearance, for which the people have a superstitious veneration. They have a mortal dread to lop off, or cut any part of it, and affirm, with a religious horror, that some persons, who had the temerity to hurt it, were afterwards severely punished for their sacrilege.

Irish poet William Allingham's 1850 work 'The Fairies' also mentions the perils of pulling up a thorn tree:

Is any man so daring
As dig them up in spite,
He shall find their sharpest thorns
In his bed at night.

There is also another, more sensory, reason why cutting a hawthorn was linked to misfortune. In rural England in medieval times the smell of hawthorn blossom was compared to the smell of the Black Death, which ravaged London in 1665 and killed between 75,000 and 100,000 people in the city and surrounding countryside. Scientists have since been able to identify the offending chemical responsible for this similarity: an organic compound called Trimethylamine, which is also found in animal tissue as it decays and whose presence might explain why even the non-superstitious prefer not to bring hawthorn blossom inside.

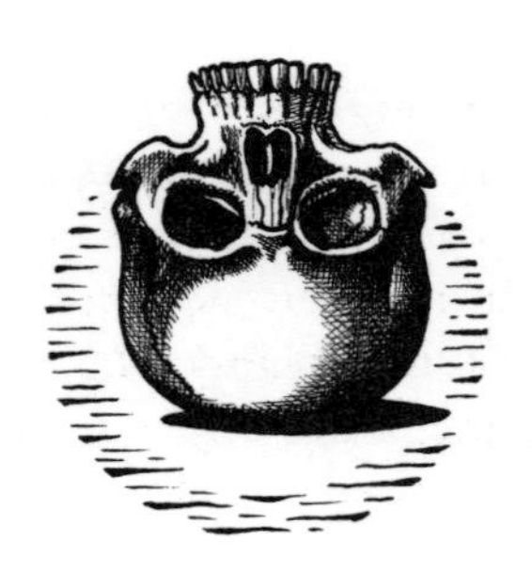

WATER DRUNK FROM A HUMAN SKULL CURES EPILEPSY

Epileptic seizures are terrifying enough for those who witness and suffer them in the modern age, but in the days before doctors had any understanding of the electrical impulses triggered in the brain, the condition was regarded with unalloyed horror. In their desperation to find a way to stop the fits, sufferers and their families were willing to try almost anything. The first mention in print of a cure involving the human skull as a drinking vessel was in Pliny the Elder's *Natural History* in AD 77: 'For epilepsy, Artemon has prescribed water drawn from a spring in the night, and drunk from the skull of a man who has been slain, and whose body remains unburnt.'

But far from being a cure that became myth, medicine derived from the human body continued to be relied upon well into the eighteenth century. The English monarch Charles II was an advocate of this grisly 'corpse medicine' and was given an extract of human skull that he had distilled in his own laboratory as he lay on his deathbed in 1685. Other high-profile advocates included the poet John Donne; Elizabeth I's surgeon John Banister, and the founding father of modern scientific analysis, Francis Bacon.

All parts of the body were used, usually distilled or ground in with other ingredients, though in official medical circles the kind of person the body parts came from didn't matter. To the superstitious practitioners searching for remedies in their own homes, however, provenance was more important. Some said that to cure epilepsy the skull had to come from a man who'd committed suicide, others agreed with Pliny that he had to have been killed by another's hand. In Central Africa, the Azande people believed that epilepsy could be cured by eating the burnt skull of a red bush monkey, because epileptic seizures caused convulsions that looked similar to the jerky movements of the monkeys.

The human skull had other medicinal uses too. In the 1600s it was common to take moss from a dead man's skull to staunch the flow of blood during a nose bleed or to cure chronic headaches, and a tooth from a skull rubbed on the gums was said to cure toothache.

NEVER SPEAK WHILE A CLOCK IS CHIMING

This superstition, still well known today, has its origins in the medieval belief that ringing bells had mysterious powers. Bells had been used in religious rituals since the classical era and their sound was thought by the Romans to scare away evil spirits. They also formed an important part of Jewish religious ceremonies, for which robes adorned with bells around the hem were worn to ward off any evil spirits lurking around the high priest's ankles. In the tenth century, churches and monasteries across Europe rang bells to call the monks to prayer, to mark the moment when a monk died and during funerals, which forged a link between pealing bells and death.

During the Great Plague of 1665 church bells rang almost constantly as they marked death after death. In the city of Tournai in Belgium, the bells were kept chiming from dawn till dusk as the plague struck, and when the townsfolk claimed victory over the disease they put it down to the power of the bells, which they thought had cleared the miasma.

From the fourteenth century onwards most towns and villages had their own clocks with a bell to chime the hour and it was in this superstitious era that stories about the prophetic power of bells originated. Folklore from almost every European country tells of bells chiming between the hours to alert people to the dangers of approaching storms, parish fires or rampaging highwaymen. In Britain, babies born as the bells were chiming were known as 'chime children' and were thought to possess healing powers, be able to see spirits and have immunity from witchcraft. If the bell chimed while a hymn was being sung it was said to be a sign of an imminent death (*see* If a Broken Clock Suddenly Chimes, There Will Be a Death in the Family).

Speaking as the bell chimed was seen as bad luck because of these connections to death; it was thought to attract the attention of evil spirits and mean that whoever had interrupted the chimes would be the next to die. In the twentieth century this idea blended with the many mystical conventions about weddings to produce a belief that if wedding vows are made during the chiming of a clock the groom will soon die. These days the severity of the superstition has thankfully lessened and chatting through the chimes will just bring run-of-the-mill bad luck.

YULE LOGS PREVENT LIGHTNING FROM STRIKING

Yule was the midwinter solstice celebrated by the Germanic pagans; it comes from the Anglo-Saxon word 'geol' and in the Northern Hemisphere falls on 21 or 22 December. For our early Scandinavian ancestors, the harsh winter conditions and months of darkness made the shortest days of the year hard to bear: food was scarce, the cold was deadly and life seemed to be ebbing from their world. For them there was no sense of certainty that the sun would return and many of the rites they practised were performed in the hope that they would appease the elements and bring a return of warmth and sunshine.

The burning of the yule log brought comfort during the depths of midwinter and provided the only source of light or heating. Usually made from a block of oak or beech, the yule log was burned all across Europe, including Russia and Siberia and even in the warmer Mediterranean. The fire was kept burning for several weeks until the days began to lengthen and during this period family and friends would gather together to tell stories, dance and sing in celebration of the return of the sun.

Christmas began to be celebrated on 25 December in the fourth century AD, and over time many of the pagan solstice traditions were absorbed by the Christian Church. From the eighteenth century onwards the yule log was traditionally lit on Christmas Eve, when it was left undisturbed in the grate all night, after which it was kept burning until Twelfth Night. The charred remains of the log were thought to possess special powers and they were used in a range of rituals designed to bring good fortune in the coming year. In France and Germany ashes from the yule were stirred into cows' feed to help them calve. In the Baltic states, the ashes are dug into the soil around fruit trees to make them more productive, and in the UK a drink made from mixing the burned wood with water was used as a cure for consumption. The belief that the blackened log should be kept in the house to prevent lightning strikes came from the old belief in sympathetic magic, a form of large-scale homeopathy where keeping a thoroughly burnt-out log meant the rest of the house was safe from burning.

IT IS GOOD LUCK IF A BABY CRIES AT ITS CHRISTENING

According to the earliest version of this superstition, which appears in print from the late 1700s, it is not only good luck for a baby to cry at its christening, but utterly essential. If it remained silent it was an omen that it would not live for long, and with infant mortality rates at around four hundred deaths per thousand births in the early eighteenth century, any hint that a child might not survive was taken seriously. Crying as the holy water was sprinkled was seen as so important that it was quite common for a nurse or mother to pinch a baby, or at least rouse it from sleep, to make sure that it made the right noises at the crucial moment.

There are two contradictory explanations for this belief; the first, common by the mid-nineteenth century, was that it was a sign that the child was too good for an earthly life and that it belonged instead with God in heaven, where, presumably, nobody cries. The second, more sinister and seemingly more widely held, was that crying was a sign that the Devil had been ousted. An entry in an 1853 edition of *Notes and Queries* explains the theory:

> ***I am inclined to suspect that the idea of its being lucky for a child to cry***

at baptism arose from the custom of exorcism, which was retained in the Anglican Church in the First Prayer Book of King Edward VI, and is still commonly observed in the baptismal services of the Church of Rome. When the devil was going out of the possessed person, he was supposed to do so with reluctance: 'The spirit cried, and rent him sore, and came out of him: and he was as one dead' (St Mark ix 26). The tears and struggles of the infant would therefore be a convincing proof that the evil one had departed.

KEEPING CATS AWAY FROM BABIES TO PREVENT THEM FROM SUCKING THE BREATH FROM A CHILD

When this superstition was first in circulation in the sixteenth century, it was thought that grown men as well as babies could be the victim of a cat's appetite for carbon dioxide. The English author William Baldwin makes reference to the notion in his satire *Beware the Cat* in 1561: 'That cat . . . got to his mouth and drew so his breath that she almost stifled him.'

Cats were believed to be the familiars of witches (*see* Black Cats), whose influence was so greatly feared in this period that any unexplained illness or ailment was put down to their evil work. Witches were also said to be able to take the form of nocturnal animals and often appeared as cats so that they could slip into people's homes without being noticed.

The precise origin of the idea that cats suck the breath of humans is difficult to pinpoint, but there was a perception that because of their links to witchcraft, cats preferred stale air that had been through someone's lungs to fresh air. Another possibility is that it was a misinterpretation of the cat's own behaviour that earned it its sinister reputation for breath sucking. Eyewitness accounts of this happening, which at the time were taken as proof of the cat's evil intent, describe cats sitting on people's chests as they sleep. This suggests that the cat's natural desire for warmth and companionship, often to be found by sitting on a warm body, might have been behind the belief. This may then have been cemented by reports of unfortunate cases where a cat might have smothered a child by curling up with it in such a way that it blocked its airways as it slept.

Either way, the belief had a strong enough hold that it lasted well into the twentieth century and is still half-believed by the most superstitious among us today, at least enough to make us shut the door of a baby's room if the cat is about, just to be on the safe side.

NEVER SPEAK ILL OF THE DEAD

This superstition has its origins in the wisdom of the ancient Greeks. The phrase first appears in print in *Lives and Opinions of Eminent Philosophers* by the third-century Greek biographer Diogenes Laërtius, who attributes it to Chilon of Sparta, one of the Seven Sages of Greece. Diogenes's work was translated into Latin in 1432 by the Italian theologian Ambrogio Traversari, whose version made the phrase well known in Latin as *De mortuis nihil nisi bonum* ('Of the dead, nothing unless good.')

English translations of Latin aphorisms were popular in the Middle Ages, when they gave a comfortingly ancient sense of order to an otherwise chaotic world. They fitted easily within the already well-established set of rules and rituals, which, coupled with the dictates of the Church, provided a moral framework for medieval life. This one, in particular, chimed with popular views about the importance of respecting the dead, whose souls were believed to stay in close contact with those they had left behind.

Before funeral homes housed 'the remains' of the dead, corpses were kept at home until they were buried, and the soul of the person was thought to hover around until that time. Even after a funeral the soul of the deceased was felt to be accessible simply by visiting the graveside. Benches were often placed among the graves so that people could sit and talk to the dead as if they were still readily able to hear them. This meant that they also believed that if someone said anything disrespectful, it would be heard by that person's spirit, which would then haunt whoever had bad-mouthed them.

These days we stick to the tradition of respecting the dead, more out of a desire to protect their memory than because we think they can hear us, although we are just as likely to say, 'I know we shouldn't speak ill of the dead but . . .' as a precursor to a bit of posthumous disparagement.

CARRYING A RABBIT'S FOOT TO WARD OFF EVIL

Rabbits' feet are well known as good-luck charms and were carried on the person or placed beside babies' cradles to ward off evil spirits, but belief in a 'lucky rabbit's foot' dates only from twentieth-century America and is in fact a blend of two much older superstitions. The idea of carrying a foot as a charm came from the belief that the foot of a rabbit or hare worked as a cure for rheumatism and digestive problems like colic and gout. This idea had its roots in medieval medicine, when the only remedies available came from plants and animals, but prevailed well into the superstition-laden sixteenth and seventeenth centuries.

The English diarist Samuel Pepys carried a hare's foot as a cure for his recurrent abdominal pains, as the following illuminating entry from 20 January describes:

> *So homeward, in my way buying a hare and taking it home – which arose upon my discourse today with Mr Batten in Westminster-hall – who showed me my mistake, that my hares-foot hath not the joint to it, and assures me he never had his colique since he carried it about him. And it is a strange thing how fancy works, for I no sooner almost handled his foot but my belly begin to loose and to break wind; and whereas I was in some pain yesterday and t'other day, and in fear of more today, I became very well, and so continue.*

The notion that such a charm could also ward off evil comes from the separate medieval belief that rabbits, whose young are born with their eyes open, had the power of second sight, so could warn people if evil spirits approached. Their renowned reproductive success also made them a symbol of fertility, which was always seen as a blessing. Saying 'white rabbits' three times on the first morning of the month was also said to bring good luck.

THE FIRST PERSON YOU SEE ON NEW YEAR'S DAY MUST BE A DARK-HAIRED MAN

Many of the rituals enacted at the start of the New Year have their roots in the Druid midwinter festival celebrations, which traditionally took place towards the end of December to mark the end of the dark days and the return of the sun. Today's fireworks and party poppers replace the singing and bell ringing used in centuries gone by to clear the air of evil spirits ready for the entrance of the New Year. The custom of drinking heavily stems from the Anglo-Saxon custom of *wassailing*, the passing on of good cheer and blessings by drinking from a shared bowl of ale.

The idea that the first person over the threshold on New Year's Day had to be male is first noted in 1805, and by 1845 the records include the fact that he must also be of a dark complexion. It was seen as unlucky if he was fair and a sign of impending doom if he should be a redhead (*see* Never Choose a Redhead as a Bridesmaid . . .). And while this is fairly recent compared with other New Year rituals, it seems to originate from a much older belief that your fortune could be affected for good or ill by the kind of person you met on the morning of any important day, such as that of a christening, wedding or the start of a long journey. The superstition appeared in this form as early as 1303 in the Middle English manuscript *Handlyng Synne* by the Gilbertine monk Robert Manning, also known as Robert de Brunne. His book was a rhyming confessional manual adapted from the *Maneul des Péchés* ('Handbook of Sins') usually ascribed to the Anglo-Norman author William of Waddington between 1250 and 1270, and which provides a rare insight into the mindset of the minor clergy and peasantry of the early fourteenth century.

Once it was established, the idea that a dark-haired man should be the first person you meet became so firmly entrenched that in Scotland it was common for suitable men to be hired by local households to pay a visit just after midnight to ensure good luck for the coming year.

NEW CLOTHES SHOULD NOT BE WORN TO A FUNERAL

As with many of the superstitions surrounding death, this one has its roots in a combination of Christian correctness and pagan ritual. In the pre-Christian era funerals were seen as beacons for evil spirits drawn by the possibility that they might be able to take possession of the corpse, so every effort was made to appease them. One method for this was to dress in old clothes that wouldn't incite their envy.

African-American tradition in the Deep South of the US said that funeral clothes or the fabric used to make them should be borrowed rather than new, because wearing new clothes would make the avenging spirit that had caused the death jealous and more likely to bring about the death of another member of the family.

There was also the possibility that the spirit of the person being buried might be envious, having so recently had their life and their ability to enjoy worldly possessions taken from them. This might cause their spirit to haunt anyone wearing new clothes (or shoes, since they would never walk the earth again.) The risk of being haunted by the ghost of the recently deceased was also the reason why black was chosen as the colour of mourning; it was believed that black clothes could confuse the ghost into seeing the wearer as a shadow, rather than a living person who could be haunted or whose body was ripe for possession.

Christianity, meanwhile, taught that for the faithful, death marked the beginning of a new eternal life, and the dressing of corpses in new clothes for burial seems also to have influenced the development of this superstition. As the seventeenth-century English scholar Joseph Bingham explains: 'We clothe the dead in new garments, to signify or represent beforehand their putting on the new Clothing of Incorruption.' So everyone attending the funeral, still mired in the sins of the earthly world, had to wear old clothes to differentiate themselves from the heaven-ready person in the coffin.

There were a number of popular variations on the theme; some claimed new clothes would wear out quickly if worn to a funeral, while others said the person wearing them would be dead by the time they wore out. These days the custom of wearing black as a mark of respect is still firmly adhered to at traditional church funerals.

A SAILOR WEARING AN EARRING CANNOT DROWN

Ear piercing is thought to be one of the oldest forms of human adornment; the oldest mummified human to be discovered by archaeologists, estimated at more than five thousand years old, has both ears pierced, and earrings are mentioned in the Old Testament and in Greek mythology. Some sources suggest that the reason sailors wear earrings is linked to ancient Greek stories about Charon, the ferryman who carried the souls of the dead across the river Styx to Hades and who had to be paid for his trouble in gold. Usually gold coins were placed in the mouths of dead bodies at burial but sailors, at risk of dying at sea and fearful of arriving without the means to pay for their passage, pierced their ears with gold rings that they could use instead.

Parallel stories exist in Christian folklore, according to which sailors wore gold earrings in the hope that they would be used to pay for a Christian burial if their bodies washed up on a foreign shore. Some sailors believed piercing their ears gave them better eyesight, while others used earrings as symbols of their experience at sea; they were said to add a gold piercing every time they traversed the globe or crossed the equator, and a black pearl earring was said to show that they had survived a shipwreck.

Because they faced almost constant peril at sea, sailors have traditionally been among the most superstitious of groups and almost every aspect of their lives, from the people on board ship to the clothes and jewellery they wore, were laced with ritual. In the Middle Ages and during the Renaissance there were no nautical maps to help them navigate or weather forecasts to warn them of storms. Many sailors in this period were at sea for war, risking their lives in battle, and those who sailed for trade were at almost as great a risk from piracy. Any protection they could find in the form of amulets or talismans against misfortune were made the most of, and the gold earring eventually came to be seen as a kind of charm against drowning. Since ear piercing was almost universal among sailors, there must have been many who proved its failings as a means of protection, but the wrath of the sea was well enough respected that few would dare to test it and the tradition continues to this day.

TO HAVE WOMEN ON BOARD SHIP MAKES THE SEA ANGRY

As this collection demonstrates, superstitions abound in every field of life, but they are present in the greatest numbers and adhered to with the most vehemence by people who feel themselves to be at the mercy of chance. Seafaring people – especially those who took to the waves in the days when most of the oceans of the world were unmapped and weather forecasting was limited to the appearance of clouds – ran a higher risk than most that life might suddenly be snatched from them, which helps explain why even those superstitions of which the origins are unclear exerted such a powerful hold.

The idea that it was unlucky to have women on board ship is thought to date back to the earliest days of seafaring and continued to be acted upon until well into the twentieth century. When Captain Collingwood, an Admiral of the Royal Navy who partnered Nelson in the Napoleonic wars, discovered in 1808 that there was a woman on board a ship in his squadron, he wrote in a letter to his colleague Admiral Purvis: 'I never knew a woman brought to sea in a ship that some mischief did not befall the vessel,' and ordered that she be sent home at the first available opportunity.

There is, however, little evidence that this drastic

step was often taken. In the Age of Sail, which spanned from the mid-sixteenth to the mid-nineteenth century, women did board ships in great numbers, and not just as passengers. Some were officially welcomed on board as the wives or mistresses of captains. Some, including many prostitutes, were smuggled aboard by officers or seaman and a few boarded ships disguised as men so they could work alongside the sailors undetected. This may have been allowed because even the most superstitious of sailors would have also been familiar with the belief that a naked woman could save lives at sea by calming the waves. This idea appears in Pliny the Elder's *Natural History*:

> *Hailstorms, they say, whirlwinds, and lightning even, will be scared away by a woman uncovering her body while her monthly courses are upon her. The same, too, with all kinds of tempestuous weather; and out at sea, a storm may be lulled by a woman uncovering her body merely, even though not menstruating at the time.*

CUTTING YOUR HAIR OR NAILS AT SEA IS BAD LUCK

In the Middle Ages cuttings of hair and nails were thought to embody the essence of a person even after they were separated from the body because they appeared to grow in a way that seemed to suggest they had a life of their own. This made them useful to witches, who were thought to be able to inflict pain on an individual simply by cursing a sample of their hair or using their nail clippings in a spell, but it also made them valuable as an offering in times of dire need. Sacrificing a living part of yourself was seen as a way of appeasing the gods in the hope that they would allow you to go on living.

This belief is ancient in origin and can be found described in a first-century Latin work of fiction *The Satyricon*, attributed to Roman author Petronius. The central character Encolpius and his lover Giton have their heads shaved at sea and their companion Hesus interprets their actions as a bad omen because of the superstition practised by sailors on the verge of being drowned of offering their hair to the gods in return for their lives. Hesus says '*audio enim non licere cuiquam mortalium in nave neque ungues neque capillos deponere, nisi cum pelago ventus irascitur.*' ('For I hear that it is not permitted to any mortal on board a ship to cut his nails or hair except while the wind and sea rage.') It is later revealed that Hesus was right to be fearful of the omen because their ship is then hit by a storm in which another of their companions is killed.

Greek legend also provides another possible source of the superstition: as symbols of life and growth, cuttings of nails and hair were used as votive offerings to Persephone, the Goddess of Spring, and it was thought that to offer these to her while at sea would anger Poseidon, the God of the Sea, and incite him to cause a storm.

RAVENS

Ravens, along with crows and other corvids (which include magpies), appear in the folklore of many European cultures; in Norse mythology a pair of ravens, Huginn and Midgard, are the familiars of the Norse god Odin and fly across the world gathering news to take back to him. In Irish legend the Morrigan, a goddess of battle, often took the form of a raven, while in medieval country lore they were usually seen as omens of death. Their jet-black feathers linked them to the night, which was dominated by witches, demons and the Devil. They were in fact often suspected of being witches who had taken on the form of a bird to allow them to spy on those they planned to harm, and seeing one perched on the roof of a house in which someone was sick was taken as a sure sign the patient would never recover. The earliest superstitious beliefs relating to ravens held them to be prophetic, though not necessarily sinister, as this extract from Virgil's *Eclogues*, from around 40 BC, describes: 'If a timely raven on my left hand . . . had not warned me at all costs to cut short this last dispute, neither your friend Moeris nor Menalcas himself would be alive today.'

By AD 77, when Pliny the Elder wrote his *Natural History* ravens were seen as 'the very worst sort of omen when they swallow their voice, as if they were being choked.' And their reputation as a minstrel of death was cemented by Shakespeare's famous reference to the bird in *Macbeth*: 'The raven himselfe is hoarse / That croaks the fatall entrance of Duncan / Under my battlements.'

One possible reason for the proliferation of the belief in rural England was the raven's cry, which was thought to sound like a cry of 'Corpse! Corpse!' Its behaviour may have contributed to its reputation too because it eats carrion and it was thought to be able to smell death. Farmers reported that if a sheep or cow was wounded ravens would often wait ominously nearby until they could settle down to feast on the carcass.

MAGPIES: ONE FOR SORROW, TWO FOR JOY

The belief that it is bad luck to see a single magpie is as prevalent today as it was in the nineteenth century, when the number of magpies seen together was used as a way to predict the future. It comes from the saying 'One for sorrow, two for joy, three for a girl, four for a boy, five for silver, six for gold, seven for a secret never to be told.' Although no specific bird is mentioned by name in the verse, it is widely understood to refer to the magpie, though in areas where magpies are rarely seen it is also applied to crows and other corvids. Passed down by word of mouth from one generation to the next, there are many regional variations of the rhyme; in America and Ireland it is more commonly recited as 'One for sorrow, two for mirth, three for a funeral, four for a birth, five for heaven, six for hell, seven's the Devil his own self.' While in Manchester there are additional lines: 'eight for a wish, nine for a kiss, ten for a surprise you should be careful not to miss, eleven for health, twelve for wealth, thirteen beware it's the Devil himself.'

These references to the Devil give a clue about the superstition's origin: according to Christian folklore, the magpie was the only bird not to raise its voice in song to comfort Jesus at his crucifixion, and Scottish legend has it that the magpie holds a drop of the Devil's blood beneath its tongue. The bird's sinister reputation may also have been linked to country people's observations of its habits, which include stealing anything shiny and killing other birds' chicks to feed its own. Certainly it was seen as a very bad omen to see one on its own and usually signified great sorrow ahead.

Various methods exist to counteract the evil influence of a lone magpie: doffing your hat, spitting over your shoulder three times or saluting it are all well documented techniques, as is greeting it with the line 'Good morning, Mr Magpie. How's your wife?', in the hope that the mention of a second bird will bring you joy instead of sorrow.

EVIL SPIRITS CAN'T HARM A PERSON STANDING INSIDE A CIRCLE

The circle is found as a symbol of completeness and eternity in many cultures and is still used symbolically in the secular world today in the familiar form of the wedding ring. The belief that the circle offers protection from evil has its roots in the ancient magic practised by the Babylonians, Assyrians and early Kabbalists, who used circles as a place of safety during incantations. They believed that the circle used could be physically realized by drawing it in salt, chalk or dust; once drawn, the circle was thought to become a metaphysical sphere, protecting its creator from all angles. The ceremonial magicians of the Middle Ages regarded the magic circle as crucial in protecting them from the influence of evil spirits who would be summoned, alongside good spirits, by their spells.

Though the Church actively discouraged the practice of magic during the medieval period, it remained an important aspect of folk religion and in many cases belief in its role was strengthened by the intense fear of the Devil so encouraged by the Church. Spells were often sought to counteract the various misfortunes that people put down to the interference of demons, or the work of the Devil, which made the protection of the magic circle even more critical. Sometimes, magicians in this era would attempt to gain heavenly protection by inscribing the names of archangels in the circle.

The modern superstition that there is safety inside a circle comes to us via the revival of magic in the late nineteenth and early twentieth centuries. Magical orders like the Golden Dawn encouraged spiritual development and ritualistic practices and had an enormous impact on the development of Occultism in the West. Some branches of contemporary paganism, particularly Wicca, still use the magic circle to harness good energy and form a protective barrier during magical rites.

IT IS UNLUCKY TO KILL AN ALBATROSS OR A GULL AS THEY CONTAIN THE SOULS OF SAILORS LOST AT SEA

This superstition has its roots in the ancient belief in metempsychosis, otherwise known as the transmigration of a soul into another living being. In the West, and especially in coastal areas, people believed that when someone died, their soul could inhabit the body of a bird. Fishermen and sailors, who faced greater perils than most while at sea and were therefore among the most superstitious of people, believed that the birds that came to fly alongside their boats carried the souls of men who had been killed at sea. This alone was enough to make killing one akin to the murder of a fellow human, but they were sacred for another reason too. The souls of the dead were thought to have the power to see both the past and the future, so their presence was seen as a warning that danger lay ahead. Seagulls containing the souls of dead sailors were said to screech before a disaster, while the mere presence of a storm petrel alongside a boat was enough to convince the living souls on board that they were in danger of drowning.

The albatross was also said to carry the soul of a dead sailor, but its presence was seen as a good omen. Its large wingspan and soaring flight made sailors believe that it brought favourable winds with it and killing one was the sin that cursed the 'Ancient Mariner' in Samuel Taylor Coleridge's famous poem of 1798:

> *'God save thee, ancient Mariner,*
> *From the fiends that plague thee thus!*
> *Why look'st thou so?' – 'With my*
> *crossbow*
> *I shot the Albatross.'*
>
> *. . . And I had done an hellish thing*
> *And it would work 'em woe:*
> *For all averr'd, I had killed the Bird*
> *That made the Breeze to blow.*

In the traditional sailing and fishing communities in Britain's coastal regions the usefulness of gulls to the community may have fuelled this superstition. The birds are scavengers, keeping the public safe by eating dead fish and fish offal that might otherwise litter the beaches and provide a breeding ground for disease. The belief in gulls as soul-birds was still alive up to at least the late nineteenth century and few fishermen would kill a gull even now.

THE CAUL OF A NEWBORN CHILD PROVIDES PROTECTION AGAINST DROWNING

The caul is a membranous part of the amniotic sac that in a small percentage of births still covers the baby's head and body as it is delivered. The sac contains the amniotic fluid that has protected and nourished the baby during its gestation, so a baby born in the caul is still surrounded by 'water.' The belief that the caul offered protection against drowning seems to have come from the observation that newborns only take a breath once free from the caul, so there is no danger of them drowning in the fluid. We now know that instinctive reflexes of a newborn allow it to close its windpipe and seal its lungs when submerged in water, but medieval science had no notion of this and people simply believed that the caul itself was responsible for protecting the baby from drowning.

This made it a precious good-luck charm for the child, and it was usually kept in a glass container or mounted on paper and framed. It also made a prized talisman for sailors, who believed it would protect them from drowning at sea. Evidence for this can be found as early as 1500 in a verse 'conceit' by 'Piers of Fulham' collected by William Carew Hazlitt in *Remains of Early English Poetry* (1866), which states the caul 'Is right a perfyte medicyne,/ Both on freshe water and on see,/ That folke shall not drowned be.'

The value placed on the caul meant that the parents of children lucky enough to be born with one often sold them to the highest bidder. This practice was made famous by Charles Dickens in *David Copperfield,* the opening chapter of which provides a fascinating insight into the semi-superstitious attitudes of early Victorian England:

> *I was born with a caul, which was advertised for sale, in the newspapers, at the low price of fifteen guineas. Whether sea-going people were short of money about that time, or were short of faith and preferred cork jackets, I don't know; all I know is, that there was but one solitary bidding, and that was from an attorney connected with the bill-broking business, who offered two pounds in cash, and the balance in sherry, but declined to be guaranteed from drowning on any higher bargain.*

A COCK CROWING AT THE WRONG TIME IS BAD LUCK

Cockerels usually crow to herald the dawn, which means they were traditionally credited with the ability to scare away the spirits of darkness. West Country wisdom said that the cockerel could see off even the Devil himself, so its call was usually welcomed as a sign that the dangers of the night had passed. When they used their voice at any other time, however, it was seen as a prophesy of danger or death. Written records of this date back to a translation of Roman author Petronius's *The Satyricon* in AD 65: 'A cock crowed . . . "It's not for nothing that yonder trumpeter has given the signal; it means either a house on fire, or else some neighbour giving up the ghost. Save us all!"'

In 1594, 'The unseasonable crowing of the barnyard cock' was listed as an ill omen in Thomas Moresin's collection *Papatus*. By the mid-1800s the crowing was said to be a specific warning that a member of the family the cock belonged to would die the next day, possibly on the exact hour that the cock had opened its beak to sing.

In Celtic and Welsh mythology a cockerel crowing three times around midnight was also believed to foretell a death, especially if it stood on the roof of a house to deliver its ominous message, as it was thought to mean that someone sleeping inside was about to meet their maker. Crowing in the early evening was less disastrous and was taken by country dwellers as a sign that there would be rain by morning, hence the old rhyme: 'If a cock goes crowing to bed, he'll certainly rise with a watery head.' The crow of a cock directly outside the door was said in rural areas to signal the arrival of a stranger, while in the Shetland Islands, your fate depended on the temperature of a cockerel's feet. If one crowed after dark and was found to have warm feet, it meant that good news was heading your way, if his feet were cold, it meant death.

CARRYING A TOADSTONE TO PROTECT AGAINST EVIL AND CURE ILLNESS

Toads and frogs were a source of fascination in ancient times because of their ability to exist on either land or water. They were seen as symbolic of the connection between the known world and the mysterious depths and were thought to possess magical powers. By the Middle Ages toads were known to produce poisonous secretions if attacked and this fact, combined with their warty skin and preference for damp, shady spots, led to their being associated with witchcraft. (*See* If a Toad or Frog Enters the House . . .) The toxins in their skin had a hallucinogenic effect and were used by witches in 'flying ointments'. At the time those using them believed the ointment actually enabled them to fly, though in fact they were simply mind-altering enough to produce the sensation of flying in anyone who ingested them. Toad secretions also made them useful to witches as a source of poison for spells designed to harm or weaken people, and one common antidote to such spells was to wear the powdered bones of a toad in a small box around the neck (*see* Wear a Toad around the Neck to Ward off the Plague).

The wearing of a 'toadstone' became popular in the

sixteenth century and in 1558 'A iewell containing a Crapon or Toade Stone set in golde' was listed among the gifts given to Queen Elizabeth in her coronation year. Though these button-shaped stones were thought to be formed in the heads of toads, they were later found to be the fossilized teeth of the Lepidotes, a Jurassic and Cretaceous bony fish that lived in both shallow seas and freshwater lakes, where toads later made their homes. The stones were worn around the neck as an amulet against a range of ailments, especially those caused by poisoning or the bite or sting of a venomous creature.

Many medieval cures were thought to work based on the principles of sympathetic magic, or the idea that like cures like. As in modern homeopathy, medicines containing an ingredient from something that could cause the same ailment was used as a cure. In this case it was hoped that a toadstone from a venomous toad would protect the wearer from the effects of any poison.

ST JOHN'S WORT GUARDS AGAINST THE DEVIL

St John's Wort has been known as a medicinal plant since ancient times and notes on its use appear in Pliny the Elder's *Natural History* in AD 77: 'The seed is of a bracing quality, checks diarrhoea, promotes urine. It is taken with wine for bladder troubles.' It was also used by the ancient Greeks and Romans to treat venomous bites, menstrual pains, upset stomachs and ulcers, as well as to combat depression or melancholy. However, it was for its spiritual powers that the plant was especially revered, as illustrated by its botanical name *Hypericum perforatum*. *Perforatum* simply means perforated, because of the tiny black 'holes' in the petals, which are actually oil secreting glands, but *Hypericum* comes from the Greek word *hyperikon*, which can be translated as 'over ghosts' (*hyper* means 'over' and *eikon* means 'apparition').

The plant's strong odour (often compared to turpentine)

was partly responsible for this belief, as it was thought that the scent would act like an incense to drive off evil spirits.

A poem said to date from 1400 reveals medieval attitudes towards the plant:

St John's Wort doth charm all witches away
If gathered at midnight on the saint's holy day.
Any devils and witches have no power to harm
Those that gather the plant for a charm:
Rub the lintels and post with that red juicy flower
No thunder nor tempest will then have the power
To hurt or hinder your houses: and bind
Round your neck a charm of similar kind.

In the thirteenth century St John's Wort is described as '*herba demonis fuga*' in a compendium of drugs compiled by the Salernitan physicians (from the celebrated medical school of Salerno in Italy, established at the end of the first century) and was later given the name '*fuga demonum*' or devil's scourge, because of its perceived power to protect people from the demons that haunted them. As medical understanding of psychological disorders grew during the scientific revolution of the Renaissance, people continued to use the words 'demons' to describe feelings of melancholy and the plant is now commonly used in the treatment of depression.

IF A PICTURE FALLS OFF THE WALL, THE PERSON DEPICTED WILL SOON DIE

Death omens are among the most common superstitions, dealing as they do with the one thing that most people fear above all else, and death omens that are unmistakably directed at an individual are the most sinister of all. This belief has been popularly held since at least the seventeenth century, though the anxieties behind it date back much further. Images of the person are viewed with suspicion in many cultures; some devout Muslims, Amish people, Native Americans and Aborigines prefer not to have their pictures taken, the former because they view it as wrong to replicate anything made in the image of God, the latter because of an ancient belief that it steals a part of their soul. This notion has parallels in Christian folklore too, in which the image of a person reflected in a mirror was believed to capture the person's soul. (*See* Breaking a Mirror.)

Stories in which such an omen had ended in the person's death were passed down from one generation to the next as confirmation of its truth. The following instance was a particularly spine-chilling example; William Laud, the Archbishop of Canterbury from 1633 to 1645 and supporter of King Charles I in the English Civil War, was famously beheaded for treason. A 1668 biography of him, *Life of William Laud* by ecclesiastical author Peter Heylin, tells the following, often repeated tale:

> *Going into his upper study . . . he [Laud] found his Picture at full Length, and taken as near unto the life as the Pensil was able to express it, to be fallen on the Floor, and lying flat upon its face, the string being broke by which it was hanged against the wall. At the sight whereof . . . he began to fear it as an Omen of that ruine which was coming toward him.*

ACKNOWLEDGEMENTS

Thanks to Heather Rhodes, John Rhodes, Annette Hibberd and Matt Hibberd, Aubrey Smith for his atmospheric drawings, and to Toby Buchan and the editorial and design team – in particular, Ana Bježančević, Dominique Enright, Glen Saville and Andrew John – at Michael O'Mara Books.

BIBLIOGRAPHY

Barrette, Elizabeth, Blake, Deborah and Duga, Ellen, *Llewellyn's 2011 Magical Almanac: Practical Magic for Everyday Living*, Llewellyn Publications, 2011

Bingham, Joseph, *The works of the learned Joseph Bingham, M. A.* (printed for Robert Knaplock, 1726), e-book digitized by Google

Brewer, Ebenezer Cobham, *A Dictionary of Phrase and Fable: Giving the derivation source, or origin of common phrases, allusions, and words that have a tale to tell*, Cassell, 1905

Connor, Catherine, *Petronius the Poet: Verse and Literary Tradition in The Satyricon*, Cambridge University Press, 1998

Defoe, Daniel, *A Journal of the Plague Year* (first published 1722), Penguin Library edition, 1966

Delys, Claudia, *A Treasury of Superstitions*, Gramercy, 1997

Flexner, Stuart and Doris, *Wise Words and Wives' Tales: The origins, meanings and time-honoured wisdom of proverbs and folk sayings olde and new*, Avon Books, 1993

Frazer, Sir James G., *The Golden Bough: A Study in Magic and Religion* (twelve volumes, 1890–1915), Touchstone, 1995

Guiley, Rosemary Ellen, *The Encyclopedia of Witches and Witchcraft*, second edition, Facts On File, 1999

Jeay, Madeleine and Garay, Kathleen, eds, *The Distaff Gospels: A First Modern English Edition of Les Évangiles des Quenouilles*, Broadview Press, 2006

Krämer, Heinrich and Sprenger, Jakob, *The Malleus Maleficarum of Heinrich Kramer and James Sprenger* (original publication *c.* 1486), unabridged online republication of the 1928 edition by the Windhaven Network, Inc., 1998–2001

Oliver, Harry, *Black Cats and April Fools: Origins of Old Wives' Tales and Superstitions in Our Daily Lives,* John Blake, 2006

Opie, Iona and Tatem, Moira, *Oxford Dictionary of Superstitions,* Oxford University Press, 2005

Origin of Superstition, 1935 US radio presentation in thirty-nine episodes; no details given, but available from the Old Time Radio website: http://www.otrcat.com/origin-of-superstition-p-1692.html; mp3 format

Pickering, David, *Cassell's Dictionary of Superstitions,* Cassell, 2003

Planer, Felix E., *Superstition,* Prometheus Books, 1988

Potter, Carole, *Knock On Wood: An Encyclopedia of Superstition,* Longmeadow Press, 1991

Puckett, Newbell Niles, *Folk Beliefs of the Southern Negro* (first edition, 1926), Kessinger Publishing, 2003; e-book or download available on the Internet Archive: http://archive.org/details/folkbeliefsofsou00puck

Quigley, Christine, *The Corpse: A History,* McFarland & Co., 2005

Radford, E. and Radford, M. A., *The Encyclopedia of Superstitions,* ed. and rev. by Christina Hole, MetroBooks, 2002

Rappoport, Angelo S., *Superstitions of Sailors,* Gryphon Books, 1928

Roud, Steve, *A Pocket Guide to Superstitions of the British* Isles, Penguin Books, 2004

Sax, Boria, *The Mythical Zoo: An Encyclopedia of Animals in World Myth, Legend, and Literature*, ABC-CLIO, 2001

Sikes, Wirt, *British Goblins: Welsh Folk-Lore, Fairy Mythology, Legends and Traditions*, J. R. Osgood & Co., 1881

Smith, Stephen Anthony and Knight, Alan (eds), *The Religion of Fools?: Superstition Past and Present* (conference: Colchester, 2005), Oxford University Press, 2008

Thompson, C. J. S., *The Hand of Destiny: Everyday Folklore and Superstitions, 1862–1943*, reprint edition, Senate, 1995

Watson, Rev. Samuel, *The Clock Struck One, and Christian Spiritualist: being a synopsis of the investigations of spirit intercourse by an Episcopal bishop, three ministers, five doctors, and others at Memphis, Tenn., in 1855* (first edition John P. Morton and Co., 1873), digitized paperback edition, BiblioBazaar 2009

Watts, Donald, *Elsevier's Dictionary of Plant Lore*, Academic Press, 2007

INDEX